EMERGENCY TELEPHONE NUMBERS

Doctor _____

Doctor _____

Doctor _____

Poison Control
   Center _____

Hospital
   Emergency
   Room _____

Paramedics _____

Fire Department _____

Police Department _____

Ambulance _____

Parents
   at Work _____

Neighborhood
   Pharmacy _____

24-Hour Pharmacy _____

Electric Company _____

Gas Company _____

Neighbor _____

Relative _____

          _____

          _____

          _____

          _____

The
American Medical Association's
Handbook
of First Aid and
Emergency Care

The
American Medical Association's
Handbook
of First Aid and
Emergency Care

**Developed by the
American Medical Association**

Medical Advisors:
Gail V. Anderson, M.D.
Christine E. Haycock, M.D.
Stanley M. Zydlo, Jr., M.D.

Text by Martha Ross Franks
Illustrations by Richard Lowe

Random House   New York

Library of Congress Cataloging in Publication Data

American Medical Association.
    The American Medical Association's handbook of first aid and emergency care.

    1. First aid in illness and injury. 2. Medical emergencies. I. Franks, Martha Ross. II. Title.
[DNLM: 1. First aid—Handbooks. 2. Emergencies—Handbooks. WA292 F834a]
RC86.7.A47 1980   616.02'52   80-5310
ISBN 0-394-73668-0

Manufactured in the United States of America
98765432
First Edition

For information about use of this book for your club or organization, contact Dept. FT, 4–6, Random House, Inc., 201 East 50th Street, New York, NY 10022

The first-aid procedures included in this book, if followed carefully, will enable the reader to deal with a wide range of emergency situations. Whenever possible, however, the reader should consult a physician.

MEDICAL ADVISORS

Gail V. Anderson, M.D., is Director of the Department of Emergency Medicine at Los Angeles County–University of Southern California Medical Center, and Professor and Chairman of the Department of Emergency Medicine at University of Southern California School of Medicine.

Christine E. Haycock, M.D., is Associate Professor of Surgery and Chief of the Division of Trauma at the College Hospital Unit of the College of Medicine and Dentistry of New Jersey Medical School of Newark. She is a Fellow of the American College of Surgeons and is a founding member of the University Association of Emergency Medical Services.

Stanley M. Zydlo, Jr., M.D., is Director of the Department of Emergency Medicine and Director of the paramedic training program at Northwest Community Hospital in Arlington Heights, Illinois. In addition, he is chairman of the board of Medical Emergency Service Associates (MESA), a corporation.

ACKNOWLEDGMENTS

Many individuals have given generously of their time, talent and knowledge to the preparation of this book, and we are deeply indebted to all of them. In addition to Drs. Gail V. Anderson, Christine E. Haycock and Stanley M. Zydlo, whose contributions to our work are beyond measure, we wish to express our special thanks to Gerald C. Crary, M.D., of the University of Southern California School of Medicine, Los Angeles, California, whose highly perceptive comments and always constructive suggestions have added so materially to the caliber of the manuscript.

We are also deeply grateful to the following individuals for their valuable help in the research for this book: Edward Almandarz (Chicago, Illinois); Frederick C. Blodi, M.D. (Iowa City, Iowa); Janet Boyes (Glen Ellyn, Illinois); Laura Brenner (Chicago, Illinois); Peter Brusca, M.D. (Wheaton, Illinois); Sandra De-Dera (Riverside, Illinois); Ronald G. Eriksen, M.D. (Carol Stream, Illinois); Gerald Feldman, D.D.S. (Milwaukee, Wisconsin); Daniel X. Freedman, M.D. (Chicago, Illinois); Chris Garrett (Chicago, Illinois); Henry C. Gonzalez (Los Angeles, California); Robert W. Herbst, M.D. (San Diego, California); Robert Kerlan, M.D. (Los Angeles, California); William Roach, M.D. (Chicago, Illinois); Findlay E. Russell, M.D. (Los Angeles, California); Edward Senay, M.D. (Chicago, Illinois); Mark Vasu, M.D. (Grand Rapids, Michigan); Willis Wingert, M.D. (Los Angeles, California). Also the Rocky Mountain Poison Center (Barry H. Rumack, M.D., Director).

To Gail Winston, C. A. Wimpfheimer, and Klara Glowczewski of Random House, our sincere thanks for their knowledgeable guidance, steadfast support and continuous encouragement.

We also want to express our appreciation to the following members of AMA's editorial team whose creativity, skill and dedication to excellence have been

vii

crucial to the quality and substance of the manuscript: Martha Ross Franks, Richard Lowe, Carole A. Fina, Ralph L. Linnenburger, Kathleen A. Kaye and Sophie Klim. And to Marie Moore, our gratitude for her dedication and proficiency in typing the manuscript.

June 1980

Charles C. Renshaw, Jr.
Editorial Director
American Medical Association
Consumer Book Program

CONTENTS

PREFACE

When we Americans think about our investments, our thoughts usually focus on money. This is natural, but it is also very short-sighted.

Surely the most valuable asset we have, both as individuals and as a nation, is our health. Good health is the cornerstone of almost every productive human activity. And yet all too often we squander it, either by neglecting our physical and emotional needs or by indulging in habits that are patently harmful.

In recent decades, our failure to adequately maintain our health has been largely obscured by the fanfare surrounding the introduction of a host of new "wonder drugs" and an imposing array of advanced medical technology. But these innovations, despite the many benefits they have brought us, are no longer adequate, by themselves, to meet our health needs and aspirations. Something more is required; something important.

It is now clear beyond any doubt that if we Americans wish to continue to enjoy the attributes of good health in the years ahead, the impetus will have to come from each of us, working as individuals in our own best interests. As individuals, each of us is better qualified than anyone else to act as the guardian of his or her health. By looking within ourselves and adopting prudent health habits and sensible life styles, we can prevent unnecessary illness, needless loss of vitality and premature old age or death.

There is, moreover, a special economic urgency about all this; an urgency that affects every one of us. Inflation has pushed medical costs—and family medical bills—to unprecedented levels. Certainly one of the most effective ways the individual can combat this numbing inflation is to avoid the avoidable and prevent the preventable.

These are the reasons that have motivated the American Medical Association, in collaboration with Random House, to publish this book. It is the first of a series of books, to be called the *American Medical Association Home Health Library,* which will bring you the latest, most authoritative and useful information available on a wide range of health care subjects. As doctors, we firmly believe that if you are given the facts, and the professional guidance necessary to understand and apply those facts, you will act wisely in your own behalf.

This emergency care book is not, in a strict sense, concerned with health maintenance; rather, it deals with those unexpected mishaps and misfortunes that, from time to time, befall nearly all of us. We have decided, nonetheless, to publish it as our first book because it embraces the widest range of physical problems that people commonly encounter. Furthermore, if you will take a little time to study the book, you will gain a valuable understanding of some of the basic facts about your body and the way it functions.

The practice of medicine is an art as well as a science, and it is thus susceptible to varying opinions regarding the exact procedures that should be followed in any individual case. Nonetheless, we are confident that the emergency care procedures recommended in this book reflect the highest standards of scientific accuracy and reliability.

Let me add just one final thought: we look upon this book, and the ones that will follow it, as an important opportunity to talk directly with you, the individual consumer of health and medical care services. We believe that once you are equipped with sound and balanced information, you will be able to shape a better, more fruitful life for yourself and those closest to you. That is certainly our hope.

James H. Sammons, M.D.
Executive Vice President
American Medical Association

Part I

HOW TO USE THIS BOOK

When an emergency strikes, first-aid treatment in the first few minutes can often mean the difference between life and death. Knowing what to do while reacting quickly and calmly before medical help arrives will enable you to provide the best care for the victim, whether it be yourself or someone else. In other instances, where an injury or illness is minor, knowing what to do and when to seek medical assistance can save needless telephone calls or unnecessary visits to the doctor and unnecessary expense as well.

This book is designed to meet your immediate needs in emergency situations and to provide you with quick and easy access to this information. In order for you to find this information easily and quickly, this book is divided into two parts.

The first part consists of general information that should be read *now* before an emergency strikes. By reading these sections *now*, and by following the suggestions that are made and familiarizing yourself with certain methods and techniques, you will be better prepared to handle an emergency when one arises.

Part I has eight general informational parts:

(1) How to Use This Book
(2) Preparing for an Emergency
(3) Life-Death Situations
(4) Loss of Limb
(5) Alarming Symptoms
(6) First-Aid Techniques to Learn and Practice
(7) When to Call a Doctor
(8) Ambulance Services and Hospital Emergency Rooms

Part II is designed for quick, easy access at the time of the emergency and includes the step-by-step treatment of specific injuries and illnesses. These injuries and illnesses, such as Abdominal Pain, Broken Bones, Heart Attack, Stroke, Vomiting, etc., are listed in alphabetical order so that they can be found quickly.

In case your name for an injury or illness is different than ours, we have included a system of guideposts to ensure your quick access to the proper entry. It works like this: If you look up "Stomachache" you will find "See Abdominal Pain," which is the master entry for this symptom. Or if you look up "Fracture," you will find the reference to its master entry, "See Broken Bones." This system is very similar to the yellow pages of your telephone book. Take a few minutes to familiarize yourself with the system by looking under the examples given above (and under others that will occur to you) and follow through to the correct master entry.

Most of the alphabetical listings are organized with detailed *step-by-step* instructions. A few entries, however, such as Chills, Fever, Miscarriage, and Muscle Aches and Pains, provide *general information* about the subject with recommendations on what you should do.

To help point out and clarify the step-by-step medical instructions that you should follow in an emergency, certain terms are repeated throughout the alphabetical listing of entries. These terms are located to the left of the instructions. The meaning of these terms and how they appear are as follows:

ABCs   A reminder to maintain an open airway and restore breathing and circulation if necessary. (See the detailed description on pages 11–15.)

Tilt head backward to maintain an open airway.

SYMPTOMS   A listing of certain conditions such as pain, nausea, swelling, etc., that indicate a certain injury or illness may exist.

IMMEDIATE TREATMENT   Treatment for a serious condition such as Choking, Third-Degree Burns, Heart Attack, etc., that must be begun *as soon as possible* before medical help arrives to prevent death or to decrease the severity of the injury.

CONTINUED CARE   Treatment that is begun only *after* the Immediate Treatment has been successfully carried out. This care often includes prevention of shock and making the victim comfortable.

WHAT TO DO   Treatment for less serious injuries, such as scrapes, bruises, blisters, etc. Often no further medical attention is needed unless problems arise that are explained in the instructions.

BEWARE   A warning that careful judgment and great care must be used with certain techniques such as applying a tourniquet or rescuing a victim from drowning.

SEE ALSO   A listing at the end of each entry of other injuries and illnesses that are directly or indirectly related. This cross reference can provide you with additional information or refer you to another injury, if you are uncertain of the victim's injury or illness.

Illustrations accompany many of the instructions for clarity.

Continue reading the first section of this book and familiarize yourself with the structure of the instructional procedures in Part II so that you and your family can be prepared for an emergency if one should occur.

In order to expedite reading and comprehension of the critical information in this book, all references to "he/she" or "him/her" will be written as "he" and "him."

The convenient shape and size of this book allow you to carry it with you wherever you go. You may want to keep a copy in the glove compartment of your car, in your fishing box, tennis bag, purse, knapsack, suitcase while traveling, and, of course, in a prominent place in your house or apartment.

PREPARING FOR AN EMERGENCY
MEDICAL CHART

One of the first things you should do is fill in (for each family member) the medical chart provided at the end of this book. The chart provides medical information you and doctors or paramedics need in an emergency, such as known allergies and vaccination dates.

There is also a place for important emergency telephone numbers in the front of the book. *Do this now,* before you forget.

KNOW THE ROUTE TO THE HOSPITAL

Know the best route to the nearest hospital emergency room. If an ambulance or paramedic team is not available, you may have to drive yourself or a victim to the hospital. It is a good idea to make a practice run so that the roads will be familiar to you at the time of the emergency. Wrong turns can take precious minutes and could mean the difference between life and death.

EMERGENCY MEDICAL IDENTIFICATION

Wearing an emergency I.D. bracelet or necklace or carrying an emergency information card could save the life of one who is unable to speak for himself after a serious accident. This medical identification is particularly important for one who suffers serious conditions such as diabetes, epilepsy, glaucoma, or hemophilia, or who has serious allergic reactions to certain medications such as penicillin or to insect stings.

These bracelets, necklaces and cards include the information you specify, such as the individual's name, address, blood type and any serious conditions or allergies. They should be worn or carried at all times. The bracelet or necklace is generally better than a card since it is more easily noticed on the victim than a card that is carried in a purse or wallet. These items are available through several manufacturers.

Ask your doctor, hospital emergency room or local medical association where you might order these. In the meantime, you can make your own card. Include your name, address, telephone number, name and telephone number of a relative to contact, your doctor's name and number, your vaccination dates, any serious medical conditions, medication taken regularly, allergies and any other important information. Be sure the card is prominently displayed in your purse or wallet.

SUPPLIES TO HAVE ON HAND IN YOUR HOME AND CAR

Now is the time to assemble those basic items you may need when an injury or illness occurs in your home, car, while camping, etc. Keep these items together in a box or other container in your home, car, boat, etc., and out of the reach of small children. Be sure to check the supplies periodically and replace used items. If a member of your family has special needs, check with your doctor for those additional items you may need. Listed below are the supplies you should have on hand.

(1) Roll of gauze bandage.
(2) Sterile gauze pads packaged separately in sealed wrappers (nonstick type).
(3) Band-aids®.
(4) Butterfly bandages.
(5) Roll of adhesive tape (1-inch size).
(6) Scissors.
(7) A 3-inch elastic bandage (for wrapping sprained ankles and wrists, etc.).
(8) Package of cotton-tipped swabs.
(9) Roll of absorbent cotton.
(10) Aspirin (regular strength, not extra-strength varieties).
(11) Children's aspirin for children under 12 years of age.
(12) Oral and rectal thermometers.
(13) Small jar of petroleum jelly to use with rectal thermometer.
(14) Bottle of Syrup of Ipecac (to induce vomiting if poisons are swallowed).
(15) Tweezers.
(16) Safety pins.
(17) Small bottle of hydrogen peroxide (3 percent solution).
(18) Calamine lotion.
(19) Bar of plain soap.
(20) Flashlight (particularly for car, boat or when camping).
(21) Snakebite kit (especially for camping).

EVERYDAY ITEMS IN YOUR HOME THAT CAN BE USED IN AN EMERGENCY

Certain everyday items in your home can be used in an emergency. It is important to be able to recognize these items for their potential emergency use. Below is a sampling of them and their uses. Keep in mind other items in your home that can also be used.

(1) Disposable or regular diapers: To use as a compress to control heavy bleeding; bandages; padding for splints.
(2) Sanitary napkins: To use as compress to control heavy bleeding; bandages; padding for splints.
(3) Towels, sheets, linens: To use as a compress to control heavy bleeding; bandages; padding for splints; emergency childbirth.
(4) Diaper pins: As pins for bandages or for a sling.
(5) Blankets: To keep victim warm.
(6) Magazines, newspapers, umbrella, pillow: As splints for broken bones.
(7) Table leaf, old door: As stretcher for head, neck and back injuries.
(8) Fan: To cool heatstroke victim.
(9) Large scarf or handkerchief: As an eye bandage or a sling.

KNOW WHAT IS NORMAL ABOUT YOURSELF

How do you know when you or someone in your family has a fever, rapid pulse, dilated pupils, etc.? The best way to find out is to first know what is normal about yourself and the other members of your family. Individual temperatures vary; and a slight fever in one person may not indicate a fever in someone else. Remember, temperatures and pulse rates have different meanings for children and adults. Infant temperatures are taken rectally and are one degree higher than oral.

The average normal temperature taken by mouth is 98.6°F (37°C). Rectal temperatures usually are one degree higher than normal oral temperatures. To find out what is normal for you, take your temperature when you know that you are not sick, at the same time of the day (temperatures can vary throughout the day) over a period of several days. This should give you an idea of what is normal for you. If your normal temperature varies slightly from the av-

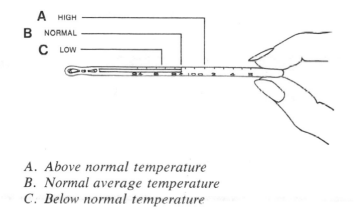

A. *Above normal temperature*
B. *Normal average temperature*
C. *Below normal temperature*

erage, write it down by your name on the medical chart so everyone in the family will know. (See also the entry on Fever in Part II for additional information on high fevers and how to take a temperature.)

The average normal pulse rate for an adult at rest is between 70–72 beats per minute. Individual pulse rates vary, of course, and can differ slightly above or below the average. Rates can also vary if one is excited or after activity. To find your normal pulse rate, place the fingertips of your second and index fingers of one hand at your wrist just below the thumb on the palm side of your other hand. Count the pulsations for 60 seconds. This is your pulse rate. Be sure to do this when you are restful and quiet, not after activity or emotional excitement.

Pulse rates in children vary according to age. The average pulse rate for a newborn infant is about 120 beats per minute. To find the pulse rate in infants, check below the left nipple. A child's pulse rate can be anywhere between 60–90 beats per minute. The older child has an average pulse rate of 80.

Dilated (very large) or constricted (very small) eye pupils can indicate a medical problem. To recognize these conditions in yourself or someone else you first need to know how normal pupils look. The best way to do this is to look at your own eyes in a mirror. Normal eye pupils are fairly small. Dilated pupils cover a good deal of the iris (colored part of the eye), while constricted pupils are about the size of a pinhead.   (*Illustration on next page.*)

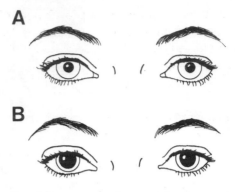

The pupils of the eye are located in the center of the iris.
A. Normal eye pupils (dark circles) are fairly small.
B. Dilated pupils (dark circles) are large and cover a large area of the iris.

COMMON SYMPTOMS AND THEIR POSSIBLE MEANING

There are several symptoms that all of us experience from time to time. They may or may not indicate a serious condition. The most common symptoms are fever, nausea and headaches.

FEVER is the body's way of indicating that something is wrong within the body. Most often it indicates that an infection is present. In some cases chills may precede a fever (see entries on Chills; Fever in Part II).

NAUSEA is a sick feeling in the stomach and is often accompanied by a desire to vomit. Nausea can be a symptom for many disorders such as appendicitis, bowel obstruction, excessive eating and drinking, allergic reactions to insect stings, spider bites, scorpion bites, snake bites, drug withdrawal, heart attack, heat exhaustion, food poisoning, early signs of pregnancy, fainting, vertigo and viral infections.

HEADACHES are most commonly caused by emotional tension. Other causes of headaches include infections, sinus infections, allergies, high blood pressure, multiple insect stings, head injuries, heat exhaustion, plant irritations, food poisoning, stroke, brain tumor and danger signals in pregnancy.

If any of these common symptoms becomes severe, persists for a long time, or is accompanied by other symptoms, medical attention should be sought.

CARDIOPULMONARY RESUSCITATION (CPR)

CPR is a basic life-support technique used in a medical crisis when the victim is not breathing and it is possible that his heart has stopped beating. The technique involves opening and clearing the victim's airway (by tilting the head backward), restoring breathing (by mouth-to-mouth or mouth-to-nose resuscitation) and restoring blood circulation (by external cardiac compression). Although opening the victim's airway and restoring breathing can be done effectively at the time of the crisis by following the instructions in this book, restoring circulation if the heart has stopped beating cannot be learned effectively on the spot. Cardiac compression must be learned through classroom instruction by qualified personnel. Practice of the technique and refresher courses are recommended. It is strongly recommended that the readers of this book take a course in CPR to learn all phases of this life-saving technique. Many communities offer qualified courses in CPR. If your community does not offer a course, call your local Heart Association or the American National Red Cross for information.

LIFE-DEATH SITUATIONS

In a crisis, certain life-saving procedures take priority over anything else. If the victim is not breathing, treatment given to other injuries will not help. Therefore, in any serious emergency, the first priority is to determine if the victim is breathing. This can be done by placing the side of your face and ear very close to the victim's mouth and nose to feel for air being exhaled by the victim. Also look to see if the victim's chest rises and falls. It is also important to determine if the victim's heart is beating (circulating blood throughout the body). This can be done by checking for a pulse at the victim's carotid artery in the neck.

A simple method of remembering the order of action to take if the victim is not breathing or his heart is not beating is the use of the term "ABCs." These letters stand for Airway, Breathing, and Circulation. They are the three basic steps in the procedure known as cardiopulmonary resuscitation (CPR).

(A) AIRWAY. In order to restore breathing, first the victim's *airway* must be clear and open. To do this:

(1) Lay victim on his back on a firm rigid surface such as the floor or the ground.
(2) Quickly clear the mouth and airway of foreign material with your fingers.
(3) If there does not appear to be any neck injury, gently tilt the victim's head backward by placing one hand beneath the victim's neck and lifting upward. Place the heel of the other hand on the victim's forehead and press downward as the chin is elevated.

(B) BREATHING. To restore breathing:

(1) Keep victim's head tilted backward.
(2) With the hand that is placed on the victim's forehead, pinch victim's nostrils using your thumb and index finger.
(3) Open your mouth widely and take a deep breath.
(4) Place your open mouth tightly around the victim's mouth and give four quick breaths. (Take a deep breath between each blow.) Continue blowing into his mouth at approximately 12 breaths per minute. Quantity is important so provide plenty of air—one breath every five seconds until you see the victim's chest rise. (Seconds are counted "one-one thousand, two-one thousand, three-one thousand," etc.)
Note:
(5) If the victim's mouth cannot be used due to an injury, remove your hand from under the victim's neck and close his mouth; then place your hand over the mouth. Open your mouth widely and take a deep breath. Place your mouth tightly around the victim's nose and blow into it. After you exhale, remove your hand from the victim's mouth to allow air to escape.
(6) Moderate resistance will be felt with blowing. If the chest does not rise, the airway is unclear and more airway opening is needed. Place hands under the victim's lower jaw and thrust lower jaw forward so that it juts out.

(*Continued on page 14.*)

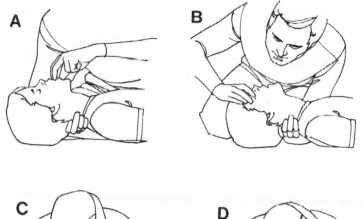

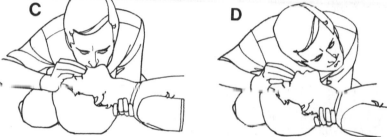

A. Lay victim on his back on a firm, rigid surface. Quickly clear the mouth and airway of foreign material.

B. Tilt the victim's head backward by placing one hand beneath the victim's neck and lifting upward. Place the heel of the other hand on the victim's forehead and press downward as the chin is elevated.

C. With the hand on the victim's forehead, pinch victim's nostrils using your thumb and index finger. Take a deep breath. Place your mouth tightly around the victim's mouth and give four quick breaths. Then give approximately 12 breaths per minute—one breath every five seconds until you see the victim's chest rise.

D. Stop blowing when the victim's chest is expanded. Remove your mouth from the victim's and turn your head toward the victim's chest so that your ear is over the victim's mouth. Listen for air leaving his lungs and watch his chest fall. Repeat breathing procedure.

(7) Watch closely to see when the victim's chest rises, and stop blowing when the chest is expanded.

(8) Remove your mouth from the victim's and turn your head toward the victim's chest so that your ear is over the victim's mouth. Listen for air leaving his lungs and watch his chest fall.

(9) If a drowning victim's stomach is bloated with swallowed water, put the victim on his stomach. To empty water, place both hands under victim's stomach and lift. After water is emptied, or if no water is emptied after approximately ten seconds, return the victim to his back.

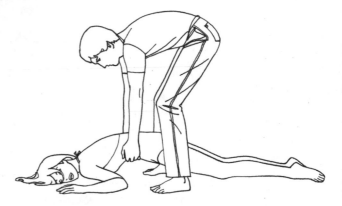

If the victim's stomach is bloated with water, put victim on stomach. To empty water, place both hands under victim's stomach and lift.

(10) Continue mouth-to-mouth breathing until victim is breathing well on his own or until medical assistance arrives.

To restore breathing in infants and children:

Mouth-to-mouth or mouth-to-nose artificial breathing is basically the same for infants and small children. However, the head should not be tilted as far back for infants and small children as for adults and large children. Place your mouth tightly over *both* the mouth and nose of the infant or small child. Breathe small puffs of air into the child's mouth and nose every three seconds (20 breaths per minute) until you see the chest rise.

(C) CIRCULATION. To restore circulation: This only should be done by those professionally trained and must be done in conjunction with artificial breathing.

In artificial breathing for children and infants, the head should not be tilted as far back as for adults and large children. Place your mouth tightly over both the mouth and nose. Breathe small puffs of air into the child's mouth and nose every three seconds until you see the chest rise.

---

(1) Check neck artery for pulse. (Check below left nipple in infants.)

(2) If no pulse is felt, begin cardiac compression. For one rescuer, give 15 compressions (80 per minute); then two quick breaths. For two rescuers, give 5 compressions (60 per minute) for every one breath. Repeat until medical assistance arrives.

Call paramedics or ambulance immediately. If this is not possible, take the victim to the nearest hospital emergency room. Have someone else drive so that you can continue artificial breathing and cardiac compression if necessary.

Most injuries and illnesses are not life-threatening. The following however, are ten medical emergencies in which the victim's life is in danger if immediate first-aid treatment is not given before medical assistance is available. It is important for you to become familiar with the immediate treatment that must be given to save the victim's life or lessen the severity of the injury. Complete step-by-step instructions for immediate treatment and continued care are also given for each of these emergencies in the alphabetical listing in Part II. Remember, medical assistance is always required with these injuries or illnesses.

1. CHOKING

If the victim is conscious:

(1) If the victim can speak, cough or breathe, *do not* interfere in any way with the victim's efforts to cough out a swallowed or partially swallowed object.

(2) If the victim cannot breathe and is standing or sitting, stand behind and slightly to one side of him and support his chest with one hand. With the heel of the other hand give four quick, very forceful blows on the back between the victim's shoulder blades.

If victim is standing or sitting, stand behind and slightly to one side of him and support his chest with one hand. With the heel of the other hand give four quick, very forceful blows on the back between the victim's shoulder blades.

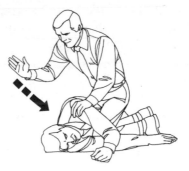

If victim is lying down, kneel beside victim and roll him onto his side so that he is facing you. Place victim's chest against your knee. With the heel of your hand give four quick, very forceful blows on the victim's back between the shoulder blades.

(3) If the victim is lying down, kneel beside the victim and roll him onto his side so that he is facing you. Place the victim's chest against your knees for support. With the heel of your hand give four quick, very forceful blows on the victim's back between the shoulder blades.

(4) If the above procedures do not dislodge the object and the victim is standing or sitting, stand behind the victim with your arms around his waist. Place your fist with the thumb side against the victim's stomach slightly above the navel and below the ribs and breastbone. Hold your fist with your other hand and give four quick, very forceful upward thrusts. This maneuver increases pressure in the abdomen which pushes up the diaphragm. This, in turn, increases the air pressure in the lungs and will hopefully force out the object. *Do not* squeeze with your arms, just use your fists.

(5) If the victim is lying down, turn him on his back. Kneel beside

(*Continued on next page.*)

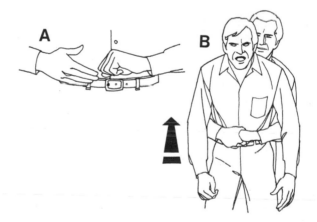

A. *Correct placement of fist with thumb side against victim's stomach slightly above the navel and below the ribs and breastbone.*

B. *If victim is standing or sitting, stand behind victim with your arms around his waist. Place your fist as shown in illustration. Hold your fist with your other hand and give four quick, forceful upward thrusts.*

the victim and put the heel of one hand on the victim's stomach slightly above the navel and below the ribs. Keep your elbows straight. Put your free hand on top of the other to provide additional force. Give four quick, very forceful downward and forward thrusts toward the head in an attempt to dislodge the object.

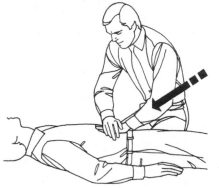

If victim is lying down, turn him on his back. Kneel beside the victim and put the heel of one hand on the victim's stomach slightly above the navel and below the ribs. Keep elbows straight. Put your free hand on top of the fist. Give four quick, very forceful downward and forward thrusts toward the head.

(6) If this gives no results, repeat the back blows and the upward abdominal thrusts until the victim coughs up the object or becomes unconscious. Look to see if the object appears in the victim's mouth or top of his throat. Use your fingers to pull it out.

If the victim is unconscious or becomes unconscious:

(1) Place the victim on his back on a rigid surface.
(2) Open the victim's airway by extending the head back. Try to restore breathing with mouth-to-mouth respiration. (See instructions on page 13.)
(3) If still unsuccessful, turn the victim on his side and give four quick, very forceful blows on his back between the shoulder blades.
(4) If still unsuccessful, turn the victim on his back and give four quick, very forceful upward abdominal thrusts. (See page 18 for conscious victim lying down.)

(5) If these procedures fail, grab the victim's lower jaw and tongue with one hand and lift up to remove the tongue from the back of the throat. Place the index finger of the other hand inside the victim's mouth alongside the cheek. Slide your fingers down into the throat to the base of the victim's tongue. Carefully sweep your fingers along the back of the throat to dislodge the object. Bring your fingers out along the inside of the other cheek. Be careful not to push the object further down the victim's throat. *Do not* attempt to remove the foreign object with any type of instrument or forceps.

(6) Repeat all of the above steps until the object is dislodged or medical assistance arrives. Do not give up!

If the victim is an infant or small child:

(1) Place the infant or small child across your forearm or lap with his head low and his face down.

(2) Give four quick blows with the heel of your hand on the child's back between his shoulder blades. Blows should be more gentle than those for an adult.

(3) If unsuccessful, turn child over onto his back and give four quick abdominal thrusts. Thrusts should be more gentle than those for an adult. (See abdominal thrusts on page 17.)

(Continued on next page.)

Place infant or small child across your forearm or lap with his head low and his face down. Give four quick blows on the child's back between his shoulder blades. Blows should be more gentle than those for an adult. (See text for abdominal thrusts if this procedure does not work.)

If victim is very fat or is pregnant:

(1) Apply four quick back blows as described on pages 16–17.
(2) Place your fist and your other hand up the middle of the breast-bone in the chest (not over the ribs) and give four quick, force-ful movements. *Do not* squeeze with your arms. Use your fists.

If you are alone and choking:

(1) Place your fist and other hand into your stomach slightly above your navel and below your ribs. Give yourself four quick, very forceful upward abdominal thrusts.
(2) Pressing your stomach forcefully over a chair, table, sink, rail-ing, etc., may also be helpful.

2. DIABETIC COMA

(1) If victim is not breathing, begin ABCs. (See pages 11–15 for in-structions.)
(2) Seek medical attention immediately, preferably at the nearest hospital emergency room.

3. DROWNING

In trying to help someone who is in danger of drowning, remember to be careful of your own safety. In deep water, a drowning person can drag his rescuer under water with him. In an emergency where you must perform the rescue, keep calm and do not overestimate your strength.

If a drowning victim is near a pier or the side of a swimming pool, lie down and give the victim your hand or foot and pull him to safety. If the victim is too far away, hold out a life-preserver ring, pole, stick, board, rope, chair, tree limb, towel or other object.

If the victim is unconscious or neck or back injury is suspected (from diving, a surfboard accident, etc.), place a board (surfboard, table leaf) under the victim's head and back while he is still in the water to keep him from moving, thus preventing further damage to the neck or back. Lift the victim out of the water on the board. This will help prevent paralysis if neck or back fracture is present.

If the victim is out from the shore, wade into the water and ex-tend a pole, board, stick, rope, etc., to the victim and pull him to safety. It may be necessary to row a boat to the victim. If so, hand

If a drowning victim is near a pier, but too far away to reach your hand or foot, lie down and hold out a pole, paddle or life preserver, and pull the victim to safety.

the victim an oar or other suitable object and pull him to the boat. If possible, the victim should hold on to the back of the boat while being rowed to the shore. If this is not possible, pull the victim carefully into the boat.

If the victim is not breathing:

(1) Begin ABCs at once, before the victim is completely out of the water and as soon as the victim's body can be supported, either in a boat or in shallow water. (See pages 11–15 for instructions.)
(2) Once out of the water, lay the victim on his back on a firm surface and continue mouth-to-mouth breathing. At this time, *do not* waste time trying to drain water from victim's lungs, although it may be necessary to do so later in the restoration of breathing procedure.

4. ELECTRIC SHOCK

It is extremely important to remain calm. There is a risk of injury to the person who is trying to help. *Do not* touch the victim directly until the electric current is turned off or the victim is no longer in contact with it. Otherwise, the first-aider risks electrocution to himself. *Victims who have been struck by lightning, however, may be touched immediately.* (Continued on next page.)

To remove the victim from the source of electricity:

(1) If possible, turn off the electric current by removing the fuse or by pulling the main switch. If this is not possible, or the victim is outside, have someone call the electric company to cut off the electricity.
(2) If it is necessary to remove the victim from a live wire, be extremely careful. Stand on something *dry* such as newspapers, a board, blanket, rubber mat or cloth, and, if possible, wear *dry* gloves.
(3) Push the victim away from the wire with a *dry* board, stick or broom handle, or pull victim away with a *dry* rope looped around victim's arm or leg. *Never* use anything metallic, wet or damp. *Do not* touch the victim until he is free from the wire.

If the victim is not breathing:

Begin ABCs at once (See pages 11–15 for instructions.) In electric shock, artificial breathing may be required for a long time. Do not get discouraged.

Be extremely careful when removing victim from a live wire. Stand on dry *area. Push victim away from the wire with a* dry *board or other* dry *object.* Never *use anything metallic or wet.* Do not *touch victim until he is free from the wire.*

5. GAS LEAK AND OTHER POISONOUS FUMES

Be extremely cautious when rescuing a victim from an area filled with smoke, chemical or gas fumes. It is best not to attempt a rescue alone. Before entering the area, rapidly inhale and exhale two or three times; take a deep breath and hold it. Remain close to the ground (crawl) while entering and rescuing the victim so that you will not inhale hot air or fumes. If the area is extremely hot or heavy with fumes, it is best for the rescuer to have an independent air supply. Do nothing but rescue the victim. Then:

(1) Get the victim into fresh air immediately.
(2) Maintain an open airway. Restore breathing and circulation if necessary. (See pages 11–15 for instructions.)
(3) Loosen tight clothing around the victim's neck and waist.
(4) Seek medical attention immediately even if the victim seems to recover completely or partially. Inform paramedics or ambulance of need for oxygen.

6. HEART ATTACK

If the victim is not breathing or is having difficulty in breathing:

Begin ABCs at once. (See pages 11–15 for instructions.)

If the victim is conscious at onset of heart attack:

(1) Gently place victim in a comfortable position. This will either be sitting up or a semisitting position. A pillow or two may allow greater comfort. Victim should not lie down flat as this position makes breathing more difficult.
(2) Loosen any tight clothing, particularly around the victim's neck.
(3) Keep the victim comfortably warm by covering his body with a blanket or coat.
(4) Calm and reassure the victim while waiting for paramedics or ambulance.

If you are alone and think you are having a heart attack:

(1) Call paramedics or ambulance immediately and inform them of a possible heart attack and of the need for oxygen.
(2) Get into a comfortable position. This will either be sitting up or a semisitting position. A pillow or two may allow greater comfort.
(3) Loosen tight clothing, particularly around your neck.
(4) Keep yourself comfortably warm.
(5) *Do not* eat or drink anything.

7. MAJOR INJURIES TO HEAD AND NECK

All head and neck injuries must be taken seriously as they can result in brain or spinal cord damage. Any victim who is found unconscious must be assumed to have a head injury until proven otherwise by medical personnel.

Head Injury

(1) Maintain an open airway. Be very careful as there may be a possibility of a broken neck. Restore breathing if necessary by mouth-to-mouth resuscitation. (See page 13 for instructions.)
(2) *Do not* move the victim more than is absolutely necessary. Handle him very carefully.
(3) Keep the victim lying down and quiet.
(4) If the victim's face is red and there is no evidence of neck or back injury (with a severe neck or back injury, victim may not be able to move arms, hands, fingers and/or legs, feet, toes; has tingling, numbness or pain in the neck or back) elevate the head and shoulders slightly with a pillow or a towel.
(5) If the victim's face is pale, keep the head level with the rest of the body.
(6) If there is no evidence of a neck or back injury, turn victim's head to the side to allow secretions to drain.
(7) Control any bleeding from the scalp by applying direct pressure.
(8) Keep victim comfortably warm.
(9) *Do not* give the victim anything by mouth.
(10) Seek medical attention promptly.
(11) If ambulance or paramedics are unavailable, take the victim to the hospital lying down. Place pads or other suitable objects on each side of the victim's head to keep it from moving.

Neck Injury

Never move a victim with a suspected neck injury without trained medical assistance unless the victim's life is in immediate danger from fire, explosion, etc. *Any* movement of the head, either forward, backward or side to side can result in paralysis or death.

(*Continued on next page.*)

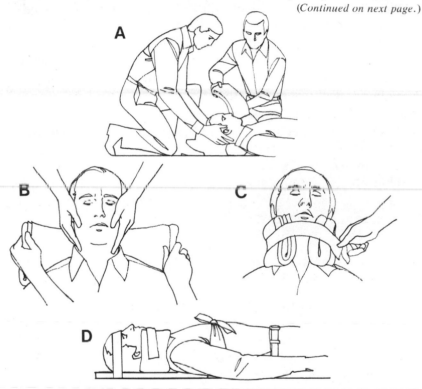

A. *If victim with suspected broken neck must be moved because of immediate danger to his life, immobilize neck with a rolled towel, etc., about 4 inches wide. Keep head as steady as possible.*

B. *Carefully wrap towel, etc., around victim's neck, keeping head as still as possible.*

C. *Tie wrap in place, being careful not to interfere with victim's breathing.*

D. *If victim is being rescued from an automobile, place a reasonably short, wide board behind victim's head and back. Tie board to victim's body around the forehead and under the armpits. Move victim slowly and gently.*

(1) If the victim must be moved because of immediate danger to his life, immobilize the neck with a rolled towel or newspaper about 4 inches wide wrapped around the neck and tied loosely in place. (*Do not* allow the tie to interfere with victim's breathing.) If the victim is being rescued from an automobile, place a reasonably short wide board behind the victim's head and back. Tie the board to the victim's body around the forehead and under the armpits. Move the victim very slowly and gently. *Do not* let the victim's body bend or twist.

(2) If the victim is not breathing or is having great difficulty in breathing, tilt his head *slightly* backward to provide and maintain an open airway. Restore breathing if necessary by mouth-to-mouth resuscitation. (See page 13 for instructions.)

(3) Summon paramedics or trained ambulance personnel immediately.

(4) Lay folded towels, blankets, clothing, sandbags or other suitable objects around the victim's head, neck and shoulders to keep the head and neck from moving. Place bricks, stones, etc., next to the blankets for additional support.

(5) Keep the victim comfortably warm.

If the victim must be taken to the hospital by someone other than trained medical personnel, then:

(1) Victim must be transported lying down on his back *face up,* unless there is danger of vomiting in which case the victim's entire body, keeping the head in the same relationship to the body as it was found, must be rolled together on its side.

(2) Place a well-padded, rigid support such as a door, table leaf, wide board, etc., next to the victim. Slide the ties under the support.

(3) If the victim is breathing on his own, hold his head so that it stays in the same relationship to the body as it was found. Other helpers should grasp the victim's clothes and *slide* the victim onto the support. Move the entire body together as a unit.

(4) *Do not lift* the victim onto the support unless there is a minimum of four helpers, preferably six.

(5) Place folded towels, blankets, cloths, etc., around the victim's head and neck to keep them from moving.

(6) Tie the victim's body to the support.
(7) Drive carefully to prevent further injury.

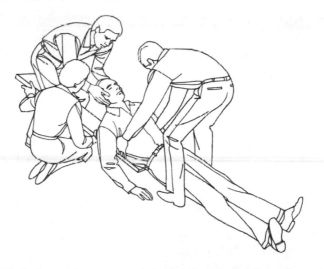

If victim with suspected back injury must be taken to the hospital by someone other than trained medical personnel, victim must be transported lying down. Place well-padded rigid support such as a door, etc., next to the victim. Victim's head must be held so that it stays in the same relationship to the body as it was found. Helpers should grasp victim's clothes and slide victim onto the support. Move entire body as a unit.

8. SEVERE BLEEDING

Direct Pressure

Direct pressure is the preferred treatment in bleeding injuries and, although it may cause some pain, constant pressure is usually all that is necessary. To apply direct pressure:

(1) Place a thick clean compress (sterile gauze or soft clean cloth such as a handkerchief, towel, undershirt or strips from a sheet) directly over the entire wound, and press firmly with

the palm of your hand. (If cloth is not available, use bare hands or fingers, but they should be as clean as possible.)

Place a thick, sterile or clean compress directly over the entire wound and press firmly with the palm of your hand. If the wound is bleeding severely, elevate the limb above the victim's heart and continue direct pressure. Do not *elevate limb if you suspect a fracture.*

(2) Continue to apply steady pressure.

(3) *Do not* disturb any blood clots that form on the compress.

(4) If blood soaks through the compress, *do not* remove the compress, but apply another pad over it and continue with firmer hand pressure over a wider area.

(5) A limb that is bleeding severely should be raised above the level of the victim's heart and direct pressure continued.

(6) *Do not* raise injured limb or neck if fracture is suspected.

(7) If bleeding stops or slows, apply pressure bandage to hold compress snugly in place.

(8) To apply pressure bandage, place center of gauze, cloth strips, necktie, etc., directly over the compress. Pull steadily while wrapping both ends around the injury. Tie knot over the compress.

(9) *Do not* wrap bandage so tightly that it cuts off circulation.

(10) Keep limbs elevated.

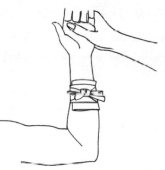

Once bleeding stops or slows, apply pressure bandage to hold compress in place. Place center of bandage directly over compress. Pull steadily while wrapping both ends around the injury. Tie knot over the compress. **Do not** *tie so tightly that it cuts off circulation. Keep limb elevated.*

Pressure Points

Pressure points should be used *only* if bleeding does not stop after the application of direct pressure and elevation. This technique presses the artery supplying blood to the wound against the underlying bone and cuts off arterial circulation to the affected area. Pressure points are used in conjunction with direct pressure and elevation of the wound above the heart.

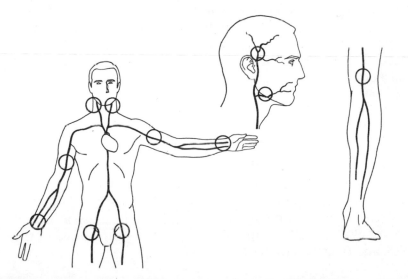

To apply pressure point to severe bleeding from the *arm:*

(1) Grasp victim's arm bone midway between the armpit and the elbow with your thumb on the outside of victim's arm and with the flat surface of your fingers on the inside of the arm where you may actually feel the artery pulsating.
(2) Squeeze fingers firmly toward your thumb against the arm bone until bleeding stops.

To apply pressure point to severe bleeding from the *leg:*

(1) Lay victim on his back, if possible.
(2) Place the heel of your hand on the front center part of the thigh, on the crease of the groin. Press down firmly. *Do not* continue the pressure point technique any longer than necessary to stop bleeding. However, if bleeding recurs, the technique should again be applied.

Tourniquet

Never use a tourniquet except in life-threatening situations where severe bleeding cannot be stopped by direct pressure on the proper point. In emergencies such as partial or complete amputation where the victim is in danger of bleeding to death, the risk of losing a limb is secondary to saving his life.

To apply a tourniquet:

(1) The tourniquet should be 2 or more inches wide and long enough to wrap around the limb twice, plus ends for tying. A strip of cloth, belt, tie, scarf or other flat material can be used.
(2) Place the tourniquet just above the wound (between wound and body), but not touching the wound. Wrap twice around the limb.
(3) Tie a half knot.
(4) Place a stick or other strong straight object on top of the half knot.
(5) Tie two full knots over the stick.
(6) Twist the stick to tighten the tourniquet until bleeding stops.
(7) Tie loose ends of the tourniquet around the stick to hold it in place. Another method of securing the stick is to use a second strip of cloth or other material to tie around the free end of the stick and then tie around the limb.

(8) *Do not* loosen or remove tourniquet once it has been applied.
(9) Attach note to victim's clothing stating location and time tourniquet was applied.
(10) *Do not* cover tourniquet.

9. SEVERE OVEREXPOSURE TO HEAT AND COLD (Heatstroke and Hypothermia)

Heatstroke (Sunstroke)

If body temperature reaches 105°F:

(1) Spray victim with hose, sponge bare skin with cool water or rubbing alcohol, or apply cold packs to the victim's body.
(2) Continue treatment until body temperature is lowered to 101–102°F.
(3) *Do not* overchill. Check temperature constantly.
(4) Dry off victim once temperature is lowered.
(5) Seek medical attention promptly, preferably at the nearest hospital emergency room.

Hypothermia (Chilling and freezing of the entire body)

(1) Maintain an open airway and restore breathing if necessary. (See pages 11–15 for instructions.)
(2) Bring victim into a warm room as soon as possible.
(3) Remove wet clothes.
(4) Wrap victim in warm blankets, towels, additional clothing, sheets, etc.
(5) Seek medical attention promptly.

10. THIRD-DEGREE BURNS

Do not remove clothes that are stuck to the burn.
   Do not put ice or ice water on burns. This can intensify shock reaction.
   Do not apply ointments, sprays, antiseptics or home remedies to burns.

(1) If the victim is on fire, smother the flames with a blanket, bedspread, rug, etc.

(2) Breathing difficulties are frequent with burns, particularly with burns around the face, neck, mouth and with smoke inhalation. Check to be sure that the victim is breathing. If not, begin ABCs at once. (See pages 11–15 for instructions.)
(3) Place cold cloth or cool water (not iced) on burns of the face, hands or feet to cool the burned areas.
(4) Cover burned area with a thick sterile dressing. A clean sheet, pillowcase, disposable diaper, etc., can be used. Keep the dressing wet if victim continues to have pain.
(5) Seek medical assistance immediately, even for a small third-degree burn.

LOSS OF LIMB

In the event that a limb such as a finger, hand, arm, toe, foot or leg is severed from the body in an accident, it is important to properly prepare and protect the limb so that it can be taken to the hospital with the victim for possible reimplantation. Severed limbs are being successfully reattached to victims, and care of the limb before reimplantation is important.

After you have cared for the victim, place the severed limb in a clean plastic bag, garbage bag or other suitable container. This keeps the limb from drying out and prevents contamination from germs.

Next, pack ice around the limb on the *outside* of the bag to keep the limb cold. The ice must not touch the limb directly; the limb should not soak in ice or water. If a second bag or container is available, the ice should be placed in this bag. Then place the bag with the limb into the bag of ice, thus keeping the limb from direct contact with the ice. Keeping the limb cold decreases its need for oxygen.

Call the hospital to notify them of a victim with a severed limb. In case the hospital is not equipped to perform surgical reimplantation, they often can make arrangements and direct the victim to a hospital that is able to perform this procedure. Also, the hospital will be able to prepare for the reimplantation and the victim.

When possible, the limb should be taken with the victim to the hospital. It is important, however, to remember that the first concern is the victim and the second concern is the limb.

ALARMING SYMPTOMS

Certain symptoms can be more frightening to experience or watch than they are dangerous to the victim. Among these symptoms are convulsions in children, epileptic seizures, fainting and headaches. The presence of these symptoms does not always indicate a critical condition. This does not mean, however, that these symptoms should be ignored. All severe or prolonged symptoms should be reported to a doctor. Try to remain calm so that you do not frighten the victim.

Convulsions (seizures) in children are most commonly caused by a rapid rise in temperature due to an acute infection. These convulsions (called febrile convulsions) seldom last longer than two to three minutes. Although more frightening to watch than dangerous, all febrile convulsions should be reported to a doctor. (See entry on Convulsions in Part II.)

Epileptic seizures usually occur in people who have an hereditary tendency to have convulsions. The seizures occur when brain cells temporarily become overactive and release too much electrical energy. The primary aim of the first-aider is to prevent the victim from harming himself. After the seizure is over, it is best to consult the victim's doctor. (See entry on Convulsions in Part II.)

Fainting is a brief loss of consciousness due to a temporary reduced blood supply reaching the brain. Recovery usually occurs within a few minutes. Here again, the first-aider wants to keep the victim from hurting himself. If recovery does not seem complete within a few minutes, seek medical attention. (See entry on Unconscious in Part II.)

Headaches are a very common complaint. They are often caused by emotional tension. Any severe or persistent headache, however, requires medical attention. (See entry on Headaches in Part II.)

FIRST-AID TECHNIQUES TO LEARN AND PRACTICE

Dressings, bandages, slings and splints are an important part of first-aid care. It is a good idea to learn and practice their application before an emergency strikes. Knowing how to apply a dressing, bandage or splint will enable you to do so more calmly and expertly during a stressful situation.

DRESSINGS

A dressing, or compress, is a covering placed directly over a wound. Its purpose is to help control bleeding, absorb secretions from the wound and prevent contamination by germs. Because the dressing is placed directly over the wound, it should be sterile. Sterile dressings such as gauze pads and Band-aids® are individually wrapped and are available at most drug stores. If a sterile dressing is not available, a clean and freshly ironed (heat from an iron helps kill germs) handkerchief, pillowcase, sheet or other cloth can be used. If time allows, a cloth boiled in water for 15 minutes and then dried will provide a sterile dressing. Items such as absorbent cotton or adhesive tape should never be applied directly to the wound as they can stick to the wound and become difficult to remove.

The dressing should be large enough to cover an area one inch beyond all edges of the wound, in order to prevent contamination of any part of the wound. To apply the dressing to the wound, hold the dressing directly over the wound and lower into place. *Do not slide or drag the dressing over the skin as this contaminates the dressing.* Discard any dressing that has slipped out of place before it has been bandaged.

BANDAGES

A bandage is a piece of material that holds a dressing or splint in place. Because a bandage does not come into direct contact with the wound, it does not need to be sterile, but it should be as clean as possible.

To function properly, a bandage must be applied snugly but not too tightly. A bandage applied too tightly can cut off circulation and cause serious tissue damage. An elastic bandage, though very effective if applied properly, can be particularly dangerous because of the first-aider's tendency to stretch it too tightly. Remember that an injured area may swell, causing the bandage to become too tight.

When applying a bandage to the arm, hand, leg or foot, leave the fingertips or toes exposed so that danger signals such as swelling, bluish or pale color, or coldness can be observed. If any of these signs appear or the victim complains of numbness or tingling, loosen the bandage immediately.

Types of Bandages

I. Band-Aids® and butterfly bandages
Band-Aids® and butterfly bandages are used for simple cuts and abrasions and can be purchased at most drug stores. Band-Aids® and butterflies are a combination of both dressing and bandage. It is important not to touch the gauze dressing while applying the bandage in order to prevent contamination. Butterfly bandages are particularly useful with small cuts as they hold the edges of the cut together. This allows the edges of the skin to grow back. When applying a butterfly bandage, gently hold the edges of the cut together.

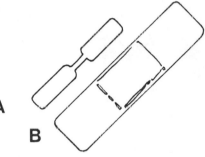

A. *Butterfly bandage*
B. *Band-Aid®*

II. Roller gauze bandage
The roller bandage comes in various widths and lengths and is usually made of gauze. It comes packaged in rolls and can be used on most parts of the body. If commercial roller bandages are not available, a bandage can be made from a clean strip of cloth. The most common uses of roller gauze are for circular, figure-of-eight and fingertip bandages.
A. Circular bandage
Circular bandages are the easiest to apply. They are used on areas that do not vary much in width such as the wrist, toes and fingers.

To apply a circular bandage:

(1) Anchor the bandage by placing the end of the gauze at a slight angle over the affected part and making several circular turns around the wrist, etc., at the same spot to hold the end in place.

(2) Make additional circular turns by overlapping the preceding strip by approximately three-fourths of its width. Continue the bandage in the same direction until the dressing is completely covered.

(3) To secure the bandage cut the gauze with scissors, etc., and apply adhesive tape or a safety pin to the bandage. Or, tie a

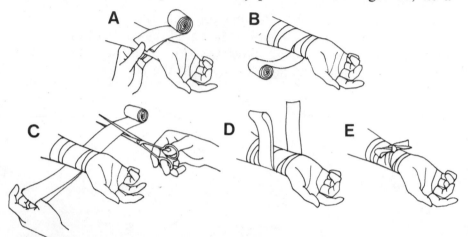

A. Anchor bandage by placing end of gauze at a slight angle over affected part and making several turns around the wrist at the same spot.

B. Make additional turns by overlapping the preceding strip by approximately three-fourths of its width. Continue the bandage in the same direction until dressing is completely covered.

C. To secure bandage, cut gauze and apply tape or safety pin, or tie loop knot by rolling gauze out about 8 inches away from part bandaged. Place thumb in the middle of the rolled gauze and pull that section of the gauze (from finger to gauze roll) back under wrist to opposite side of arm. If scissors are available, cut gauze.

D. Double gauze on one side and single gauze on the other.

E. Tie knot over the bandage.

loop knot by extending the rolled gauze out about 8 inches away from the part being bandaged. Place the thumb or two fingers in the middle of the rolled out gauze and pull that section of the gauze (from the fingers to the gauze roll) in the same direction as you did in applying the bandage. The remainder of the gauze and roll will be on the opposite side. Now, with the doubled gauze on one side and the single gauze on the other, tie a knot over the bandage. If scissors are available, cut off unused gauze.

B. Figure-of-eight bandage

A figure-of-eight bandage is particularly useful for the ankle, wrist and hand. To apply a figure-of-eight bandage:

(1) Anchor the bandage with one or two circular turns around the foot, etc., as described in circular bandage.

(Continued on next page.)

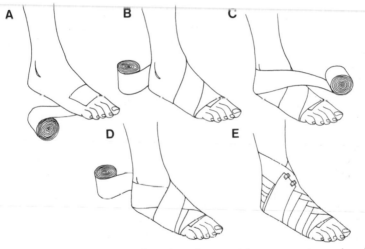

A. *Anchor bandage with one or two circular turns around the foot.*
B. *Bring bandage diagonally across the top of the foot and around the ankle.*
C. *Continue bandage down across the top of the foot and under the arch.*
D. *Continue figure-of-eight turns, with each turn overlapping the last turn by about three-fourths of its width.*
E. *Bandage until the foot (not toes), ankle and lower leg are covered. Secure bandage with tape or clips.*

(2) To make the figure-of-eight, bring the bandage diagonally across the top of the foot, around the ankle, down across the top of the foot and under the arch. Continue these figure-of-eight turns, with each turn overlapping the preceding turn about three-fourths of its width. Bandage until the foot (not toes), ankle and lower part of the leg are covered.

(3) Secure the bandage with tape, clips, or safety pins, or tie off as described for circular bandages.

C. Fingertip bandage

The fingertip bandage is particularly useful when the fingertip itself is injured. To apply this bandage:

(1) Anchor the bandage at the base of the finger with a few circular turns as described for circular bandages.

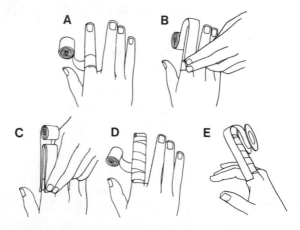

A. Anchor bandage at base of finger with several circular turns.

B. Hold bandage down at the base where it is anchored. Bring bandage up the front of the finger, over fingertip and down back side to base of finger.

C. Hold down bandage at the base with the thumb. Repeat the back-and-forth bandaging process over the fingertip until several layers cover the finger.

D. To hold bandage in place, start at base of finger, and make circular turns up the finger and back to the base.

E. To secure bandage, apply piece of tape about 6 inches long up side of finger, across tip and down other side of finger.

(2) With the index finger of one hand, hold the bandage down at the base where it is anchored. Bring the roll of bandage up the front of the finger, over the fingertip and down the back side to the base of the finger.

(3) Now, with the thumb, hold down the bandage at the base and repeat the back and forth process of bandaging over the fingertip as described. Repeat bandaging until several layers cover the finger.

(4) Next, starting at the base of the finger, make circular turns up the finger and back to the base to hold the bandage in place.

(5) To secure the bandage, apply a piece of tape approximately 6 inches long up the side of the finger, across the tip and down the other side of the finger. Or, tie off as described in circular bandage.

III. Triangular bandage

The triangular bandage has many uses in an emergency. It can serve as a covering for a large area such as the scalp, as a sling for a broken bone, or can be folded into a cravat and used as a circular or figure-of-eight bandage. A triangular bandage is usually made of muslin but other material can be used. It can be easily made at home. To make a triangular bandage, cut a piece of cloth 36 to 40 inches square. Next cut the fabric diagonally from corner to corner. Now you have two triangular bandages.

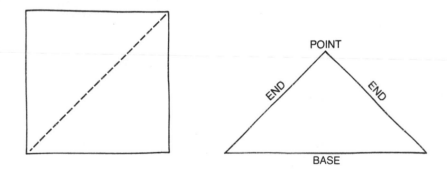

A. Sling

(1) Place one *end* of the bandage over the uninjured shoulder so that the *base* and other *end* of the triangle hang down over the chest. Place the *point* under the elbow of the injured arm.

(2) Elevate the hand about four inches above the level of the elbow.
(3) Lift the lower end of the bandage up over the other shoulder and tie the two ends together at the *side* of the neck.
(4) Fold the point forward and pin it to the outside of the sling.
(5) *Do not* cover the fingers with the sling.

A. *Place one* end *of the bandage over uninjured shoulder. The* base *and other* end *of triangle hang down over the chest. Place* point *under the elbow of uninjured arm.*
B. *Elevate hand about 4 inches above level of elbow. Lift lower end of bandage up over other shoulder and tie two ends together at the* side *of the neck.*
C. *Tie at neck.*
D. *Fold point forward and pin to outside of sling.*
E. *Completed sling with point folded and pinned to outside of sling. Leave fingers exposed.*

B. Head bandage

(1) Place the center of the base of the triangle across the forehead so that it lies just above the eyes. The point of the bandage should lie down the back of the head.
(2) Bring both ends above the ears and around to the back of the head. Just below the lump at the back of the head, cross the two ends over each other snugly and continue to bring the ends back around to the center of the forehead.
(3) Tie the ends in a knot.
(4) Tuck the point hanging down the back of the head in the fold where the bandage crosses in the back.

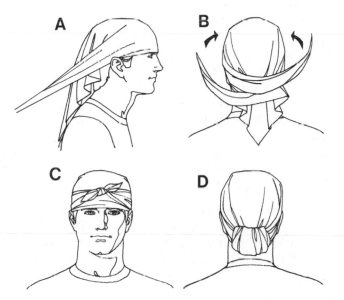

A. Place center of triangle base across forehead so that it lies just above the eyes, with point of bandage down the back of the head. Bring ends above the ears and around to back of head.
B. Cross the two ends snugly over each other just below the lump at the back of the head. Bring ends back around to center of forehead.
C. Tie ends in a knot.
D. Tuck point in fold where bandage crosses.

C. Cravat (Necktie)

The triangular bandage can be folded as a cravat bandage and then used as a circular or figure-of-eight bandage. To fold as a cravat:

(1) Fold the point of the bandage over to the middle of the base.
(2) Continue to fold the bandage lengthwise along the middle until the bandage is the desired width.

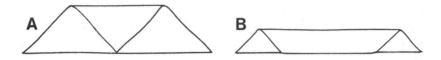

A. *Fold point of triangle bandage to middle of base.*
B. *Continue folding lengthwise along the middle until bandage is desired width.*

SPLINTS

Splints are used to keep the injured part from moving. They ease pain and help to prevent shock.

Objects that can be used for splinting include boards, straight sticks, brooms, pieces of corrugated cardboard bent to form a three-sided box, rolled newspapers or magazines, pillows, rolled blankets, oars, umbrellas, etc. The splint should extend beyond the joint above and the joint below the broken bone.

Padding such as cloth, towels, blankets, etc., should be placed between the splint and the skin of the injured part.

Splints can be tied in place with neckties, strips of cloth torn from shirts, handkerchiefs, belts, string, rope or other suitable material.

Do not tie the splint so tightly that the ties interfere with circulation.

Swelling or bluish discoloration in the fingers or toes indicates that the ties are too tight and need to be loosened. Also loosen splint ties if the victim experiences numbness or tingling, or if he cannot move his fingers or toes. Check wrist or ankle for pulse and loosen if no pulse can be felt.

To splint specific broken bones, see entry on Broken Bones in Part II.

WHEN TO CALL A DOCTOR

At some time you may need to call a doctor about an injury or other medical problem. If the problem is a real emergency such as a broken bone, severe bleeding, possible heart attack or stroke, diabetic coma, severe abdominal pain, etc., the victim should be taken to the hospital by paramedics and/or an ambulance. After you have done all you can for the victim, call the victim's doctor, if possible, to inform him of the emergency.

If you are unsure of the victim's condition and the victim has severe or prolonged symptoms such as pain, vomiting and/or diarrhea (particularly with blood), difficulty in breathing, high fever, etc., call the doctor regardless of the hour. However, if the illness or injury is not severe, try to call the doctor during his office hours.

You may have to tell your problem to a nurse if the doctor is seeing a patient. But the doctor, or the nurse with the doctor's instructions, will get back to you. If you must call the doctor at home, do not wait until late at night unless the victim's situation is considerably worse, in which case you should call at any hour. If the victim is seriously injured or becomes ill on a Friday and you are unsure of what to do, do not wait to call the doctor over the weekend as he may not be as readily available; call him immediately.

It is very helpful when calling the doctor to give him specific information regarding the victim's symptoms such as temperature, pulse rate, number of loose watery stools in a given number of hours, location of pain, age of the victim and any other symptoms of the illness or injury.

AMBULANCE SERVICES AND HOSPITAL EMERGENCY ROOMS

It is necessary to call an ambulance to take a victim to a hospital emergency room anytime the victim's symptoms are critical or life-threatening—severe head, neck, or back injury, anaphylactic shock, drug overdose, unconsciousness, etc. In these instances the victim should be transported to the hospital as quickly as possible.

Most communities have some type of ambulance service available. The most highly trained and specialized personnel are paramedics (technically known as EMT-paramedics). They are trained to administer advanced life-support techniques along with cardio-pulmonary resuscitation (CPR), to take electrocardiograms, to give medication and to apply splints for broken bones, etc. Many ambulances with paramedics have telemetry equipment hooked up to a local hospital that relays a doctor's instructions to the paramedics.

Emergency medical technicians (EMTs) can provide CPR and other procedures such as splinting broken bones. They cannot, however, administer medication or perform sophisticated medical procedures.

Finally, there are ambulance services that offer little more than transportation to the hospital. The drivers of such vehicles are not trained to perform emergency care beyond a simple bandaging. This does not mean that they do not serve a purpose for those who have no other transportation to the hospital.

Paramedics and other ambulance personnel are usually available through various community resources such as the fire department, police department, private sectors and funeral homes. Check with the resources in your community to find out what is available *before* an emergency strikes so that you will know the type of service to call.

Paramedics should not be called for minor illnesses or injuries such as sprained ankles, minor cuts, colds, etc.; they need to be available for people who have more serious conditions. Often victims with minor injuries can be driven to the hospital by a family member or friend.

It is difficult to answer the question "When do you go to the emergency room?"

Anytime the victim's symptoms are critical or life-threatening, he must be taken to the hospital. In other instances, any situation that seems like an emergency to you warrants a trip to the emergency room. No one can say what constitutes an emergency to another person, so if you will feel relieved by going to the emergency room, then you should go.

If you are taking someone to the hospital and there is time, call ahead to the emergency room. Tell them you are coming and the nature of the victim's injury or illness. This enables the emergency-room staff to know what to expect and to prepare for the victim's arrival.

When the victim arrives at the hospital, be prepared to wait if the emergency room is busy, unless the victim's condition is critical. The most serious and critical cases will be seen first. Any specific information the victim or someone else can give the emergency-room staff about the victim's condition will help the staff determine the seriousness of his condition. Specific complaints, such as severe crushing chest pain or sharp lower abdominal pain, are very helpful information. Other useful information includes:

(1) When symptoms began.
(2) What makes pain or condition better or worse.
(3) What victim was doing when injury or illness occurred.

Certain other information about the victim will be needed by the hospital personnel. If time allows before leaving for the hospital, gather insurance identification cards, Medicare or Medicaid cards, or any other medical benefits to which the victim is entitled. Also, take along any medication the victim is currently taking. This information can be very helpful to the doctors. Be prepared to give the victim's name, age, address, a history of major injuries or illnesses, and known allergies.

Laboratory tests and x-rays may be necessary and take time. These tests help confirm the investigative work of arriving at a diagnosis so that treatment can be given.

Depending on the size and the location of the hospital, most emergency rooms can offer full medical services ranging from bandaging a cut to surgery. If the emergency room cannot handle a specific situation, it usually can arrange to send the victim to another hospital.

Emergency-room treatment is generally more expensive than medical treatment received in a doctor's office. Most emergency rooms must be staffed with doctors, nurses and other personnel on a 24-hour basis, and this is expensive. Also, emergency rooms must be equipped with costly equipment.

Most hospitals will process insurance forms. More hospitals are also accepting major credit cards for payment.

Part II

ABDOMINAL PAIN

There are hundreds of causes of abdominal pain. Some are quite serious and require immediate medical care. If symptoms are severe, regardless of whether they fall into any of the following categories, seek medical attention promptly. A victim of severe abdominal pain should never be given an enema, laxative, medication, food or liquids (including water) without a doctor's order since doing so may aggravate the problem or cause a complication.

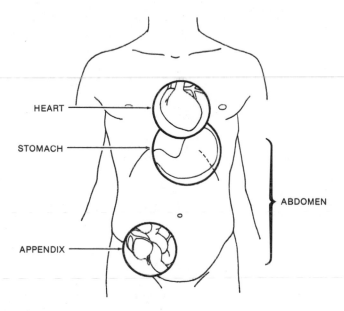

HEART

STOMACH

ABDOMEN

APPENDIX

The abdomen is the part of the body located between the diaphragm and the pelvis. It includes such organs as the liver, stomach, gall bladder, intestines and appendix. The heart lies outside of the abdomen.

APPENDICITIS

Appendicitis is a surgical emergency. It results when the appendix becomes inflamed and infected. Immediate surgical removal of the appendix is necessary.

SYMPTOMS

(1) Pain usually begins intermittently in a generalized area around the navel and later moves to the lower right part of the abdomen where it may become constant. Pain is not always severe.

(2) Fever may be present.

(3) Nausea and vomiting.

(4) Loss of appetite.

(5) Possible diarrhea, constipation or any change in bowel habits.

(6) Tenderness in the abdomen, especially the right lower quarter when touched, or when pressing on the area and releasing rapidly.

(7) Any one or all of the above may be present. In children, only a few symptoms, such as lack of appetite and tender abdomen, may be present.

Do not give victim laxatives, enemas, medication, food or liquids (including water).

IMMEDIATE
TREATMENT

Seek medical attention promptly, preferably at the nearest hospital emergency room. Delay can be serious.

BOWEL OBSTRUCTION

A bowel obstruction is the complete or partial interference in the passing of waste materials through the bowels. This may be caused by adhesions (scar formation) following surgery, abscess, tumors or twisted bowels. Bowel obstruction is a surgical emergency.

SYMPTOMS

(1) Severe cramplike pain in the abdomen that subsides and then repeats.

(2) Nausea and vomiting.

(3) Abdomen expands and becomes firmer than normal.
(4) Diarrhea, constipation or any change in bowel habits.
(5) Any one or all of the above may be present.
    Do not give victim laxatives, enemas, medication, food or liquids (including water).

IMMEDIATE TREATMENT   Seek medical attention promptly, even with the slightest suspicion of bowel obstruction.

MENSTRUAL CRAMPS

Cramping pains in the mid-lower abdomen are common during menstruation. They occur at the beginning of the period and may last for several days.

WHAT TO DO   (1) If there is no doubt that pain is caused by menstrual cramps, mild pain relievers such as aspirin or those products (also containing aspirin) specifically made for menstrual cramps are often helpful.
(2) If pain is severe or persists, or is greater than usual, medical attention is needed.

TUBAL PREGNANCY

A tubal pregnancy is a pregnancy that develops outside of the uterus. Most of these pregnancies develop in the Fallopian tubes. As the embryo grows, it becomes too large for the narrow Fallopian tube. Rupture of the tube usually occurs during the second or third month of pregnancy. A ruptured Fallopian tube is a surgical emergency because excessive internal bleeding into the abdomen can occur, leading to shock or death.

SYMPTOMS   (1) Menstrual period is late, prolonged or missed.
(2) Pain on one side of the lower abdomen, which

may not be severe until Fallopian tube rup-
tures.

(3) Vaginal bleeding may occur prior to, or with,
abdominal pain.

(4) Victim may become pale.

(5) Pulse may be rapid.

(6) Pain may be also present in the shoulder area.

(7) Any one or all of the above may be present.

Do not give victim laxatives, enemas, medication, food or liquids (including water).

**IMMEDIATE
TREATMENT**

Seek medical attention promptly as surgery is
probably necessary.

ABDOMINAL PAIN IN INFANTS AND CHILDREN

Abdominal pain is not unusual in children. Almost all children experience a stomachache at
some time. A stomachache is usually not serious
if it lasts less than an hour and there are no other
symptoms such as fever, cough, headache, vomiting or diarrhea. Whenever in doubt about symptoms, seek medical advice, especially if symptoms increase in frequency and severity.

In certain situations, abdominal pain can indicate a serious condition. Seek medical attention
promptly if pain is severe, lasts longer than an
hour or if the abdomen is tender to touch or feels
rigid. Also seek medical help if a fever, cough,
headache, vomiting or diarrhea are present.

Do not give the child laxatives, enemas, medication, food or liquids (including water).

Abdominal pain in infants can be very serious
and needs medical attention. An infant usually indicates abdominal pain by crying loudly, bending
his legs and drawing his knees toward his chest.
Seek medical attention promptly, preferably at
the nearest hospital emergency room if vomiting,

abdominal swelling or diarrhea containing mucus or blood is present, as an acute emergency may exist.

Do not give the infant laxatives, enemas, medication, food or liquids (including water).

See Also: Diarrhea; Miscarriage; Poisons (food); Pregnancy, Danger Signs; Vomiting; Wounds (abdominal)

● **Aches:** see Ear Injuries and Earaches; Headache; Muscle Aches and Pains; Sprains; Strains

● **Addiction:** see Drug Abuse

● **Alcohol abuse:** see Drug Abuse

● **Allergic reactions:** see Bites and Stings; Poisons; Rashes; Shock; Unconscious; Vomiting

● **Allergies:** see Asthma; Croup; Headaches

● **Ambulance services:** see Part I, pages 43-45

● **Amputation:** see Part I, page 32

● **Anaphylactic shock:** see Bites and Stings (insect stings); Shock (shock from reaction to insect stings)

● **Animal bites:** see Bites and Stings (animal)

● **Ankle injury:** see Broken Bones and Spinal Injuries; Sprains

● **Ant bites:** see Bites and Stings (insect stings)

● **Apoplexy:** see Stroke

● **Appendicitis:** see Abdominal Pain (appendicitis)

● **Arm injury:** see Broken Bones and Spinal Injuries

● **Arteries:** see Bleeding

● **Artificial respiration:** see Drowning; Electric Shock; Heart Attack; Unconscious.

ASTHMA

Asthma is a condition resulting from an irregular, gradual or sudden narrowing of the airway bronchial tubes, causing difficulty in breathing, especially on exhaling. Often, but not always, an attack results from exposure to something to which the victim is allergic. Infections, colds, changes in the weather or emotional factors can also lead to an attack.

SYMPTOMS
(1) Difficulty in breathing out (exhaling).
(2) Difficulty in breathing out, with a wheezing or whistling sound as air is released.
(3) Nervousness, tenseness, fright.
(4) Coughing.
(5) Possible perspiration on forehead.
(6) Possible vomiting.
(7) Possible slight fever.
(8) Bluish tinge to skin in severe attacks due to lack of oxygen.
(9) Victim always tries to sit upright as it is easier for him to breathe.
(10) Choking sensation.
(11) Any one or all of the above may be present.

WHAT TO DO
If this is the first episode of suspected but undiagnosed asthma, seek medical attention. Report all details of the attack. If a doctor cannot be reached, take victim to the nearest hospital emergency room. Comfort and reassure the victim, particularly a child who may be frightened by the experience, since emotional stress may make the condition worse. Keep victim in a sitting position.

If attacks have occurred before, give victim prescribed medications according to his doctor's instructions. Do not give victim anything else without physician's advice. Report the attack to the physician that day or the next day even if the victim seems well.

DANGER SIGNALS

If symptoms continue and one or more of the following happens:

(1) Failure to improve with medication.
(2) Breathing can barely be heard; possible difficulty inhaling.
(3) Inability to cough.
(4) Increased bluish tinge to skin.
(5) Pulse rate more than 120 beats per minute.
(6) Increased anxiety.
(7) Victim tries to pull up shoulders and chin to get air.

Then:
    Seek medical attention at once, preferably at the nearest hospital emergency room as this is a dire medical emergency. The victim may be near respiratory failure and could collapse.

● **Baby:** see Childbirth, Emergency

● **Back injury:** see Broken Bones and Spinal Injuries; Head Injuries; Strains

● **Balance disturbance:** see Unconscious (vertigo)

● **Bandages:** see Part I, pages 34 – 42

● **Barking cough:** see Croup

● **Bee stings:** see Bites and Stings (insect stings)

● **Benzedrine, abuse:** see Drug Abuse

● **Birth:** see Childbirth, Emergency

BITES AND STINGS

ANIMAL BITES

Animal bites can result in serious infections as well as in tissue damage. Cat bites can be particularly serious as they may cause cat-scratch fever. Many animals including bats, skunks, squirrels, raccoons, foxes, rats and dogs can transmit rabies. Tetanus is also a danger with animal bites.

WHAT TO DO   (1) Clean the wound thoroughly with soap and water for five minutes or more.
(2) Put a sterile bandage or clean cloth over the wound.
(3) Seek medical attention promptly, particularly for a bite on the face or neck.

Note:
It is very important to catch and confine any animal that has bitten someone so that it may be watched for rabies. Capture the animal alive if possible. If it is absolutely necessary to kill the animal, try to avoid damage to the head. Save the body for examination by health department officials. If the animal cannot be captured, try to remember physical characteristics and actions of the animal so that it can be identified.
Notify the police and local health department.

HUMAN BITES

Any human bite that breaks the skin needs immediate medical treatment. These bites can lead to very serious infections from oral bacteria that may contaminate the wound.

WHAT TO DO   (1) Clean the wound thoroughly with soap and water for five minutes or more.
(2) Put a sterile bandage or clean cloth over the wound.
(3) Seek medical attention promptly.
   Do not put medication, antiseptics or home remedies on the wound.

INSECT STINGS

Insect stings can be life-threatening if the victim is allergic to the insect's venom. (See Allergic Reactions to Insect Stings on pages 57–60.)

Insect stings result in more deaths yearly than result from snake bites. The most common stinging insects are bees, hornets, wasps, yellow jackets, bumble bees and fire ants.

USUAL REACTION

Symptoms occur at bite area and may last 48 to 72 hours.

(1) Pain.
(2) Local swelling.
(3) Redness.
(4) Itching.
(5) Burning.
(6) Any one or all of the above may be present.

WHAT TO DO

(1) If stung by a honey bee, carefully remove the stinger by gently scraping with a knife blade or fingernail. *Do not* squeeze with tweezers as this may result in more venom entering the body.
(2) Wash the area with soap and water.
(3) Place ice wrapped in cloth or cold compresses on sting area to decrease absorption and spread of the venom.
(4) Soothing lotions such as calamine or a paste of baking soda and a little water are often helpful in relieving discomfort.

ALLERGIC REACTIONS TO INSECT STINGS

Anaphylactic shock is a generalized total body allergic reaction.

Allergic reactions to insect stings can be life-threatening and can occur from one or more bites or stings. Allergic reactions often occur if victim has been bitten or stung previously.

SYMPTOMS

(1) Severe swelling in other parts of the body such as the eyes, lips and tongue. Severe swelling may occur at the bite site as well.
(2) Weakness.
(3) Coughing or wheezing.
(4) Severe itching.
(5) Stomach cramps.
(6) Nausea and vomiting.
(7) Anxiety.
(8) Difficulty in breathing.
(9) Possible bluish tinge to skin.
(10) Dizziness.
(11) Collapse.
(12) Possible unconsciousness.
(13) Hives or hivelike rash on body.
(14) Any one or all of the above may be present.

If emergency kit is *not* available for insect stings:

IMMEDIATE
TREATMENT

(1) Maintain an open airway and restore breathing if necessary.
(2) If stung by a honey bee, carefully remove the stinger by gently scraping with a knife blade or fingernail.
   Do not squeeze the stinger with tweezers as this may result in more venom entering the body.
(3) If the victim experiences the severe symptoms listed that suggest a severe allergic reaction *and* the victim is known to have had previous severe reactions to insect stings, the use of a tourniquet may be necessary. Although not all experts agree on this method, many allergists suggest the use of a tourniquet in severe reactions where the victim's life is at stake. Emergency insect sting kits available

only by prescription contain a tourniquet for such cases.

The tourniquet is used only if the sting has just occurred and is on the arm or leg. A rubber tourniquet works best but a strip of cloth, cord, etc., may be used.

Tie the tourniquet 2 to 4 inches above the sting toward the body. *Do not* tie so tightly that the victim's circulation is cut off completely. *Be sure* you can find a pulse below the tourniquet. Loosen the tourniquet about every five minutes until medical assistance is obtained.

(4) If the victim experiences severe symptoms of an allergic reaction but has no known previous history of severe reactions to insect stings and the sting has just occurred on the arm or

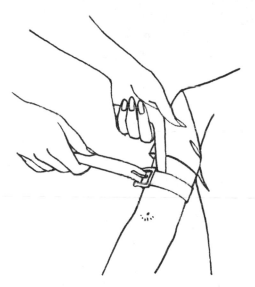

A light constricting band is used for severe reactions to insect stings *(see Insect Stings, Anaphylactic Shock in text) and for rattlesnake, copperhead and cottonmouth (not coral) snake bites. Place the hand 2 to 4 inches above the bite toward the body.* Do not *cut off circulation. You should be able to slip your finger under the band.*

leg, apply a light constricting band such as a watchband, belt, etc., 2 to 4 inches above the sting toward the body. The band *should not* be so tight that it cuts off circulation. You should be able to slip your finger under the band. *Do not* remove the band until medical assistance is obtained.

(5) Seek medical attention promptly, preferably at the nearest hospital emergency room.

CONTINUED CARE

(1) Place cold compresses on sting area to stop absorption and spread of the injected venom.
(2) Keep victim lying down unless he is short of breath; then let him sit up.
(3) Keep victim comfortable and quiet.

If emergency kit for insect stings is available:

IMMEDIATE TREATMENT

(1) Maintain an open airway and restore breathing if necessary.
(2) Remove stinger if stung by a honey bee. (See Immediate Treatment on page 58.)
(3) If victim is unable to administer an injection of adrenalin, follow instructions in the emergency kit.
(4) Seek medical attention promptly, preferably at the nearest hospital emergency room. Call paramedic rescue, if available.

CONTINUED CARE

See Continued Care above.

MULTIPLE STINGS (Toxic Reaction)

SYMPTOMS

(1) Rapid onset of swelling.
(2) Headache.
(3) Muscle cramps.
(4) Fever.
(5) Drowsiness.
(6) Unconsciousness.

(7) Any one or all symptoms may be present.

WHAT TO DO (1) Remove stingers if stung by honey bees. (See Immediate Treatment for Allergic Reactions to Insect Stings on pages 58–60.)
(2) Wash sting sites with soap and water.
(3) Place ice wrapped in cloth or cold compresses on sting sites.
(4) Soothing lotions such as calamine or a paste of baking soda and a little water are often helpful in relieving discomfort.
(5) Seek medical attention as other medication may be needed.

BLACK WIDOW SPIDER BITES

Black widow spider bites are particularly harmful to very young children, the elderly or the chronically ill.

The black widow spider *has a shiny black body. Its unique feature is a red hourglass marking on the underside of its body.*

SYMPTOMS (1) Slight redness and swelling around bite.
(2) Sharp pain around bite.
(3) Heavy sweating.
(4) Nausea and possible vomiting.
(5) Stomach cramps.
(6) Possible muscle cramps in other parts of the body.
(7) Tightness in chest and difficulty in breathing and talking.
(8) Any one or all of the above may be present.

(Continued on next page.)

IMMEDIATE
TREATMENT

(1) Maintain an open airway and restore breathing if necessary.
(2) Keep the bitten area lower than victim's heart.
(3) Place ice wrapped in cloth or cold compresses on bitten area.
(4) Seek medical attention promptly, preferably at the nearest hospital emergency room. If possible, take the spider with you.

CONTINUED
CARE

(1) Keep victim quiet.
(2) Watch for signs of shock and treat if necessary. (See Shock on pages 207–09.)

BROWN RECLUSE SPIDER BITES (Fiddler Spider)

Brown recluse spider bites are particularly harmful to very young children.

The brown recluse spider (*also called fiddler spider*) *is characterized by a dark brown violin-shaped marking on the top front portion of its body.*

SYMPTOMS

(1) Stinging sensation at time of bite.
(2) Redness which later disappears as a blister forms.
(3) During following eight hours, pain becomes more severe.
(4) Over the next 48 hours, chills, fever, nausea, vomiting, joint pains and possible rash appear.

(5) Destruction of tissue that forms an open ulcer.

(6) Any one or all of the above may be present.

IMMEDIATE TREATMENT See Immediate Treatment for Black Widow Spider Bites on page 62.

CONTINUED CARE See Continued Care for Black Widow Spider Bites on page 62.

TARANTULA BITES

Tarantula bites are not usually as serious as those of the black widow spider or the brown recluse spider.

The tarantula *is a large spider with a very hairy body and legs.*

SYMPTOMS (1) Pain usually not severe at time of bite.

(2) Severe, painful wound may develop later.

(3) Any one or all of the above may be present.

WHAT TO DO (1) Wash area with soap and water.

(2) Place ice wrapped in cloth or cold compresses on bite area.

(3) Soothing lotions such as calamine may be helpful in relieving discomfort.

(4) If severe reaction occurs, see Immediate Treatment and Continued Care for Black Widow Spider Bites on page 62.

(5) It is a good idea to seek medical attention.

MARINE LIFE STINGS

Stings from certain types of marine life are poisonous. Two of the most common offenders are the Portuguese man-of-war and the jellyfish.

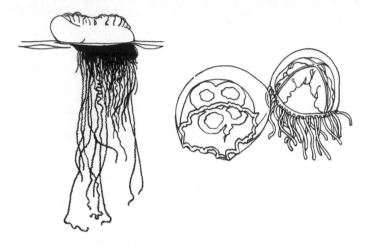

Portuguese man-of-war   *Jellyfish*

SYMPTOMS
(1) Intense burning pain.
(2) Reddening of the skin.
(3) Skin rash.
(4) Muscle cramps.
(5) Nausea and vomiting.
(6) Difficulty in breathing.
(7) Possible shock.
(8) Any one or all of the above may be present.

WHAT TO DO
(1) If stung by a Portuguese man-of-war, wrap cloth around hands to prevent stinging while carefully removing any attached tentacles. Cover tentacles with dry sand if available.
(2) Wash area with rubbing alcohol or household ammonia diluted with water. (This will sting.)
(3) Watch for signs of shock and treat if necessary. (See Shock on pages 207–09.)
(4) Seek medical attention.

SCORPION STINGS

Some species of scorpions are more poisonous than others. Scorpion stings are particularly harmful to very young children.

The scorpion *looks like a small lobster. It has a set of pincers and a stinger located in the tail which arches over its back.*

SYMPTOMS

(1) Severe burning pain at the site of the sting.
(2) Nausea and vomiting.
(3) Stomach pain.
(4) Numbness and tingling in affected area.
(5) Spasm of jaw muscles may occur, making opening of mouth difficult.
(6) Twitching and spasm of affected muscle.
(7) Shock. (See Shock on pages 207–09.)
(8) Convulsions.
(9) Possible coma.
(10) Any one or all of the above may be present. See Immediate Treatment and Continued Care for Black Widow Spider Bites on page 62.

SNAKE BITES

When you are bitten by a snake, it is important to know whether or not it is poisonous. Poisonous snakes in the United States include the rattlesnake, cottonmouth (water moccasin), copperhead and coral snake.

The rattlesnake, cottonmouth and copperhead are pit vipers and are recognized by deep pits (poison sacs) located between the nostrils and the eyes. They also have slitlike eyes rather than the

The rattlesnake *has deep poison pits located between the nostrils and the eyes. It has slitlike eyes and two long fangs. A unique feature of the rattlesnake is the set of rattles at the end of the tail.*

rounded eyes of the nonpoisonous snakes (with the exception of the coral snake). These snakes also have long fangs that leave distinctive marks followed by a row of teeth marks. Rattlesnakes get their name from a set of rattles at the end of their tail. Cottonmouths have white coloring inside their mouths.

The copperhead *also has deep poison pits between the nostrils and eyes, slitlike eyes and long fangs.*

The coral snake is a member of the cobra family. It has red, yellow and black rings. The yellow rings are narrow and *always* separate the red rings from the black. A phrase to remember that identifies the coral snake is "Red on yellow will kill a fellow, red on black won't hurt Jack." The coral

The cottonmouth, *also called water moccasin, has the same deep poison sacs between the nostrils and eyes, slitlike eyes and two long fangs as do the rattlesnake and copperhead. A distinctive feature is the white coloring inside the mouth.*

snake is smaller than the pit vipers, has rounded eyes like nonpoisonous snakes, and *always* has a black nose. Its venom is highly toxic to humans.

Unlike the rattlesnake, copperhead and cottonmouth, the coral snake *has rounded eyes. The coral snake also has fangs. Its markings consist of yellow, red and black rings with the narrow yellow rings always separating the red rings from the black. The coral snake always has a black nose.*

Nonpoisonous snakes have rounded eyes. They do not have pits between their eyes and nostrils and do not have fangs.

The triangular shaped head of the rattlesnake, copperhead and cottonmouth.

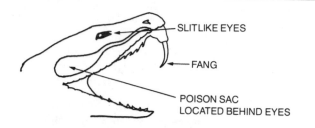

Characteristics of the rattlesnake, copperhead and cottonmouth.

Try to capture and kill the snake if possible and take it with you to the medical facility. If this is impossible, remember the characteristics of the snake.

If bitten by a rattlesnake, cottonmouth or copperhead:

SYMPTOMS

(1) Severe pain.
(2) Rapid swelling.
(3) Discoloration of the skin around the bite.
(4) Weakness.
(5) Nausea and vomiting.
(6) Difficulty in breathing.
(7) Blurring vision.
(8) Convulsions.

(9) Shock.

(10) Any one or all of the above may be present.

IMMEDIATE TREATMENT

(1) Maintain an open airway and restore breathing if necessary.

(2) Keep the affected area below the level of the victim's heart.

(3) If bitten on the arm or leg, place a light constricting band such as a belt, watchband, etc., 2 to 4 inches above the bite toward the

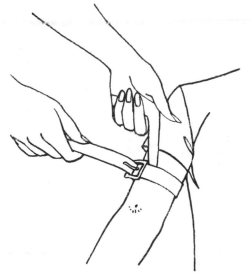

A light constricting band is used for severe reactions to insect stings *(see Insect Stings, Anaphylactic Shock in text) and for rattlesnake, copperhead and cottonmouth (not coral) snake bites. Place the hand 2 to 4 inches above the bite toward the body. Do* not *cut off circulation. You should be able to slip your finger under the band.*

body. It should not be so tight that it cuts off circulation. You should be able to slip your finger under the band. The wound should ooze.

(4) If swelling should reach the band, remove the band and place it 2 to 4 inches above the first site.

(5) *Do not* remove the band or bands until medical assistance is obtained.
(6) Wash bite area thoroughly with soap and water.
(7) Immobilize a bitten arm or leg with a splint or other suitable device.
(8) *If snake bite kit is available,* use blade provided in the kit; otherwise sterilize a knife blade over a flame. This must be done immediately after the victim has been bitten. Carefully make a one-eighth to one-fourth inch deep cut through each fang mark in the direction of the *length* of the arm or leg. The cut should not be more than one-half inch long.

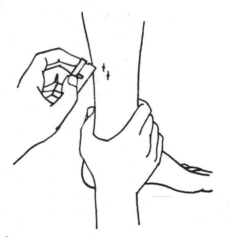

If bitten by a copperhead, cottonmouth or rattlesnake (not coral snake), immediately make a ⅛- to ¼-inch-deep cut with a sterile blade through each fang mark in the direction of the length of the arm or leg.

Do not make cross mark cuts. Be very careful not to cut any deeper than the skin as muscle, nerve or tendon damage may occur, particularly on the wrist, hand or foot.
(9) If suction cups are available, place them over victim's wound and draw out venom; otherwise use your mouth if it is free of cuts and sores.

Do not swallow venom. Spit it out occasionally. Continue suction for 30 minutes or more. If mouth method is used, rinse mouth when finished.

BEWARE

(10) *Never* use cold or ice compresses on wound as this may result in extensive tissue damage.

(11) Seek medical attention promptly, preferably at the nearest hospital emergency room. If possible, have someone telephone ahead and tell of poisonous snake bite and type of snake so that antivenom serum can be made ready.

CONTINUED CARE

(1) Cover wound with a sterile or clean bandage.

(2) Keep victim quiet, calm and reassured.

(3) Treat victim for shock. (See Shock on pages 207–09.)

(4) *Do not* let the victim walk unless absolutely necessary and if so, then slowly.

(5) Victim may have small sips of water if desired and if he has no difficulty swallowing. *Do not* give water if victim is nauseated, vomiting, having convulsions or is unconscious.

(6) *Do not* give victim alcoholic beverages.

If bitten by a coral snake:

SYMPTOMS

Some symptoms may not occur immediately.

(1) Slight pain and swelling at the site of the bite.

(2) Blurred vision.

(3) Drooping eyelids.

(4) Difficulty in speaking.

(5) Heavy drooling.

(6) Drowsiness.

(7) Heavy sweating.

(8) Nausea and vomiting.

(9) Difficulty in breathing.

(10) Paralysis.

(11) Shock. (See Shock entry on pages 207–09.)
(12) Any one or all of the above may be present.

IMMEDIATE
TREATMENT

(1) Quickly wash the affected area.
(2) Immobilize a bitten arm or leg with a splint or other suitable device. (See Splinting on pages 85–86; 93–95.)
(3) Keep the victim quiet.
(4) Seek medical assistance promptly, preferably at the nearest hospital emergency room. If possible, have someone call ahead to notify the hospital of poisonous snake bite and type of snake so that antivenom serum can be made ready.
(5) *Do not* tie off bite area.
(6) *Do not* apply cold or ice compresses.
(7) *Do not* give victim food or alcoholic beverages.

If bitten by a nonpoisonous snake:

WHAT TO DO

(1) Keep affected area below the level of the victim's heart.
(2) Clean area thoroughly with soap and water.
(3) Put a bandage or clean cloth over the wound.
(4) Seek medical attention as medication or a tetanus shot may be necessary.
See Also: Poisons; Rashes (bites and stings); Shock (shock from reaction to insect stings); Unconscious

● **Black eye:** see Eye Injuries (blunt injuries)
● **Black widow spider bites:** see Bites and Stings (insect bites)

BLEEDING

ABCs

With all serious injuries, check and maintain Airway. Restore Breathing and Circulation if necessary.

Tilt head backward to maintain an open airway.

Bleeding may be from a vein or an artery or both. Venous bleeding is dark red in color and flows steadily. Arterial bleeding is bright red in color and usually spurts from the wound. Arterial bleeding is more critical. Both can occur at the same time.

EXTERNAL BLEEDING

IMMEDIATE TREATMENT

I. Direct Pressure

Direct pressure is the preferred treatment in bleeding injuries and, though it may cause some pain, constant pressure is usually all that is necessary to stop the bleeding.

To apply direct pressure:

(1) Place a thick clean compress (sterile gauze or a soft clean cloth such as a handkerchief, towel, undershirt or strips from a sheet) directly over the entire wound and press firmly with the palm of your hand. (If cloth is not available use bare hands or fingers, but they should be as clean as possible.)

(2) Continue to apply steady pressure.

(3) *Do not* disturb any blood clots that form on the compress.

(4) If blood soaks through the compress, *do not* remove the compress but apply another pad over it and continue with firmer hand pressure over a wider area.

(5) A limb that is bleeding severely should be

(Continued on page 75.)

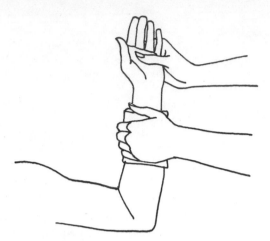

Place a thick, sterile or clean compress directly over the entire wound and press firmly with the palm of your hand. If the wound is bleeding severely, elevate the limb above the victim's heart and continue direct pressure. Do not *elevate limb if you suspect a fracture.*

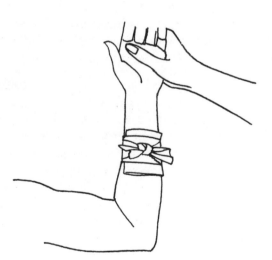

Once bleeding stops or slows, apply pressure bandage to hold compress in place. Place center of bandage directly over compress. Pull steadily while wrapping both ends around the injury. Tie knot over the compress. Do not *tie so tightly that it cuts off circulation. Keep limb elevated.*

raised above the level of the victim's heart and direct pressure continued.

(6) *Do not* raise injured limb or neck if fracture is suspected.

(7) If bleeding stops or slows, apply pressure bandage to hold compress snugly in place.

(8) To apply pressure bandage, place center of gauze, cloth strips, necktie, etc., directly over the compress. Pull steadily while wrapping both ends around the injury. Tie knot over the compress.

(9) *Do not* wrap bandage so tightly that it cuts off circulation.

(10) Keep limb elevated.

II. Pressure Points

Pressure points should be used *only* if bleeding does not stop after the application of direct pressure and elevation. This technique presses the artery supplying blood to the wound against the underlying bone and cuts off arterial circulation to the affected area. Pressure points are used in conjunction with direct pressure and elevation of the wound above the heart.

To apply pressure point to stop severe bleeding from the *arm:*

(1) Grasp victim's arm bone midway between the armpit and the elbow with your thumb on outside of victim's arm and with the flat surface of your fingers on the inside of the arm where you may actually feel the artery pulsating.

(2) Squeeze fingers firmly toward your thumb against the arm bone until bleeding stops.

To apply pressure point to stop severe bleeding from the *leg:*

(1) Lay victim on his back, if possible.

(2) Place the heel of your hand on the front center part of the thigh, at the crease of the groin. Press down firmly. *Do not* continue the pres-

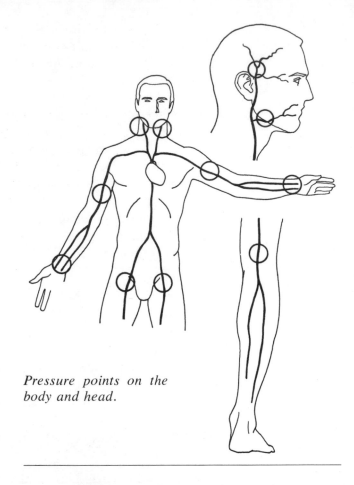

Pressure points on the body and head.

sure point technique any longer than necessary to stop the bleeding. However, if bleeding recurs, technique should again be applied.

III. Tourniquet

BEWARE

Never use a tourniquet except in life-threatening situations where severe bleeding cannot be stopped by direct pressure on the proper point. In emergencies, such as partial or complete amputation where the victim is in danger of bleeding to death, the risk of losing a limb is secondary to saving his life.

To apply a tourniquet:

(1) The tourniquet should be 2 or more inches wide and long enough to wrap around the limb twice, with ends for tying. A strip of cloth, belt, tie, scarf or other flat material can be used.

(2) Place the tourniquet just above the wound (between wound and body) but not touching the wound. Wrap it twice around the limb.

(3) Tie a half knot.

(4) Place a stick or other strong straight object on top of the half knot.

(5) Tie two full knots over the stick.

(6) Twist the stick to tighten the tourniquet until the bleeding stops.

(7) Tie loose ends of the tourniquet around the stick to hold it in place. Another method of securing the stick is to use a second strip of cloth or other material to tie around the free end of the stick. Then tie the cloth around the limb.

(8) *Do not* loosen or remove tourniquet once it has been applied.

(9) Attach a note to victim's clothing stating location and time tourniquet was applied.

(10) *Do not* cover tourniquet.

Seek medical attention immediately with any injury that is bleeding severely, particularly when a tourniquet has been applied.

CONTINUED CARE

Treat for *shock:*

(1) Keep victim lying down.

(2) Elevate victim's feet 8 to 12 inches unless the victim is unconscious, has neck, spine, head, chest, severe lower face or jaw injuries. He should be placed on his side with his head slightly extended backward (jaws opened) to prevent choking on fluids or vomit. If victim is having trouble breathing, raise his head and shoulders slightly, keeping his airway clear.

(3) If pain increases, lower feet again unless this makes victim more uncomfortable.
(4) Keep victim comfortably warm with a blanket, coat, etc., but not too warm. If possible, place a blanket beneath the victim on the ground.
(5) If medical attention is more than two hours away, give the victim water or a weak solution of salt (1 level teaspoon) and baking soda (one-half level teaspoon) mixed with 1 quart of cool water. Give an adult 4 ounces (one-half glass), a child 1 through 12 years 2 ounces, and an infant 1 ounce. Have victim sip slowly over a 15-minute period. Clear juices, such as apple juice, may also be given.

Do not give fluids if victim is unconscious, having convulsions, is likely to need surgery, has a brain injury or an abdominal wound, or is vomiting. Stop giving fluids if vomiting occurs.
(6) Look for other injuries such as internal bleeding and/or broken bones and treat them. (See Broken Bones on pages 80–98.) Treating the injury may lessen the shock.
(7) If possible, obtain information about the accident.
(8) Calm and reassure the victim. Gentleness, kindness, and understanding play an important role in treating a victim in shock.

INTERNAL BLEEDING

Internal bleeding is not always obvious. You may suspect internal bleeding if victim has been in an accident, fallen or received a severe body blow.

SYMPTOMS

(1) Vomit that resembles coffee grounds.
(2) Coughed-up blood that is bright red and/or frothy (bubbly).

(3) Stools that are black or contain bright red blood.
(4) Paleness.
(5) Cold, clammy skin.
(6) Rapid and weak pulse.
(7) Lightheadedness.
(8) Distended abdomen.
(9) Restlessness.
(10) Thirst.
(11) Apprehension.
(12) Mental confusion.
(13) Any one or all of the above may be present.

IMMEDIATE TREATMENT

(1) Maintain an open airway and restore breathing if necessary.
(2) Seek medical attention promptly.

CONTINUED CARE

(1) Treat for shock. (See treatment for shock in Continued Care for External Bleeding on pages 77–78.)
(2) *Do not* give victim anything to drink.
(3) Look for other injuries such as broken bones and treat the injury.
(4) Calm and reassure the victim.

NOSEBLEEDS

WHAT TO DO

(1) Have victim sit down and lean forward and keep his mouth open so that blood or clots will not obstruct airway.
(2) Pinch nose closed for approximately 15 minutes by the clock. Release slowly. *Do not* blow or touch nose. If bleeding continues, pinch nose closed again for five minutes. Be sure that victim is not swallowing blood.
(3) Place cold cloth or ice in a cloth against victim's nose and face to help constrict blood vessels.
(4) If bleeding continues, seek medical attention.

(5) Seek medical attention if broken nose is suspected.

(6) *Do not* irritate or blow nose for several hours after bleeding stops.

See Also: Part I, pages 27–31; Pregnancy, Danger Signs; Shock; Wounds

Blindness: see Eye Injuries

Blisters: see Burns; Ear Injuries and Earaches (frostbite); Minor Injuries (blisters); Overexposure: Heat and Cold (cold injuries); Overexposure: Heat and Cold (heat injuries); Poisons (plant irritations)

Blood clot: see Minor Injuries (injured fingertip)

Blotching of the skin: see Rashes

Blurring of vision: see Eye Injuries; Pregnancy, Danger Signs

Bone injury: see Broken Bones and Spinal Injuries; Dislocations

Botulism: see Poisons (food poisoning)

Brain damage: see Head Injuries

Breathing difficulty: see Part I pages 12 – 14; Asthma; Bites and Stings (insect bites); Choking; Convulsions (seizures); Croup; Drowning; Drug Abuse; Electric Shock; Head Injuries; Heart Attack; Poisons; Shock; Stroke; Unconscious

BROKEN BONES AND SPINAL INJURIES

BROKEN BONES

ABCs

With all serious injuries, maintain an open Airway. Restore Breathing and Circulation if necessary.

A break or crack in a bone is a fracture. A fracture may be closed or open. In a closed break or crack, the broken bone does not come through the skin. Usually the skin is not broken near the fracture site.

Tilt head backward to maintain an open airway.

In an open break, there is an open wound that extends down to the bone, and parts of the broken bone may stick out through the skin. An open break is usually more serious because of severe bleeding and the possibility of infection.

SYMPTOMS   Always suspect a broken bone if any of these symptoms appear.

(1) Victim felt or heard a bone snap.
(2) Pain or tenderness, particularly to the touch, at the site of the injury or when moving the affected part.
(3) Difficulty in moving the injured part. But the bone may be broken even if victim can easily move the injured part.
(4) Abnormal or unnatural movement of the injured part.
(5) Victim feels grating sensation of bone ends rubbing together.
(6) Swelling in the area of the injury.
(7) Deformity of the injured part.
(8) A difference in the shape or length of a bone in comparison to the same bone on the other side of the body.
(9) Bluish discoloration at the site of the injury.
(10) Any or all of the above may be present.

IMMEDIATE   There are certain guidelines and procedures to
TREATMENT   follow with any broken bone or spinal injury.

(1) Maintain an open Airway. Restore Breathing and Circulation if necessary. (See Back and Neck injuries on the following pages for specific instructions.)

(2) Stop any severe bleeding. If victim has an open break, cut clothing away from the wound.

Do not wash or stick anything, including medication, into the wound. *Gently* apply pressure with a large sterile (or clean) pad or cloth to stop the bleeding.

Do not try to push back any part of the bone that is sticking out. Cover the entire wound including the protruding bone with a bandage. Splinting an open break is the same as for a closed break. (See Splinting on pages 83–98.)

(3) Treat for shock. See specific types of broken bones on the following pages for information about moving the victim.

(4) Call paramedics or an ambulance promptly.

(5) Always suspect a broken neck or spinal injury if victim is unconscious, has a head injury, neck pain, tingling or paralysis in the arms or legs. (See Back and Neck injuries on pages 86–90; 95–97.)

(6) *Do not* move the victim, particularly if he has head, neck or spine injuries or if paramedics or other trained ambulance personnel are readily available unless the victim is in immediate danger such as fire, drowning, explosion, gas inhalation, traffic, etc. If victim must be moved, immobilize the injured part first. For example, tie the injured leg to the uninjured leg, if possible.

Do not lift a victim with a suspected neck or spinal injury out of the water without a back support, such as a board. If victim must be dragged to safety, *do not* drag him side-

ways but pull him by the armpits or legs in
the direction of the length of his body.

Do not let the victim's body bend or twist,
particularly his neck or back. (See Back,
Head and Neck injuries on the following
pages for specific instructions.)

(7) Apply splints if paramedics or other trained
personnel are not readily available and
someone else must take the victim to the
hospital. Always splint the injured part
above and below the injury before moving
the victim. (See Splinting on pages 83–98.)

(8) Handle victim very gently. Rough handling
often increases the severity of the injury.

(9) *Do not* try to set a broken bone or push a
protruding bone back into the body.

(10) *Do not* give the victim anything to eat or
drink.

SPLINTING AND OTHER PROCEDURES

Splints are used to keep the injured part from
moving. They ease pain, prevent the break from
becoming worse and help to prevent shock.

Objects that can be used for splinting include
boards, straight sticks, brooms, pieces of corrugated cardboard bent to form a three-sided box,
rolled newspapers or magazines, pillows, rolled
blankets, oars, umbrellas, etc. The splint should
extend beyond both the joint above and the joint
below the broken bone.

Padding such as cloth, towels, blankets, etc.,
should be placed between the splint and the skin
of the injured part.

Splints can be tied in place with neckties, strips
of cloth torn from shirts, handkerchiefs, belts,
string, rope or other suitable material.

Do not tie the splint so tightly that the ties interfere with circulation. Swelling or bluish discoloration in the fingers or toes also may indicate that the ties are too tight and need to be loosened. Also loosen splint ties if victim experiences numbness, tingling or if he cannot move his fingers or toes. Check wrist or ankle for pulse and loosen ties if no pulse can be felt.

The following are instructions on how to splint and treat breaks of specific bones.

Ankle

WHAT TO DO
(1) Keep victim lying down.
(2) Remove victim's shoes.
(3) Place pillow (preferably) or rolled blanket around the leg from the calf to well beyond the heel so that the pillow edges meet on top of the leg.
(4) Tie pillow in place.

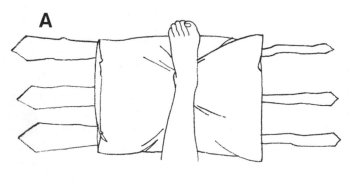

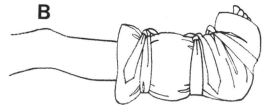

A. Remove victim's shoes. Place pillow or rolled blanket and ties around the leg from the calf to well beyond the heel.

B. Tie splint in place. Fold ends of pillow that extend beyond the heel so that it supports the foot.

(5) Fold ends of pillow that extend beyond the heel so that it supports the foot.

Upper Arm

WHAT TO DO
(1) Place some light padding in victim's armpit.
(2) Gently place arm at victim's side with lower arm at a right angle across victim's chest.

(Continued on next page.)

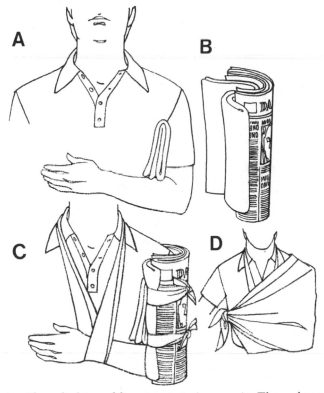

A. Place light padding in victim's armpit. Then place arm at victim's side with lower arm at a right angle across victim's chest.
B. Padded splint using newspaper.
C. Place padded splint to outside of upper arm and tie in place above and below the break. Support lower arm with a narrow sling tied around the neck.
D. Bind upper arm to victim's body by placing large towel, etc., around splint and victim's chest and tying under opposite arm.

(3) Apply padded splint to outside of upper arm and tie in place above and below the break.

(4) Support the lower arm with a narrow sling tied around the neck.

(5) Bind upper arm to victim's body by placing a large towel, bed sheet, cloth, etc., around the splint and the victim's chest and tying under opposite arm.

(6) Victim is usually more comfortable sitting up while riding to the hospital.

Lower Arm and Wrist

WHAT TO DO
(1) Carefully place the lower arm at a right angle across the victim's chest with the palm facing toward the chest and the thumb pointing upward.

(2) Apply a padded splint on each side of the lower arm, or use folded, padded newspapers or magazines wrapped under and around both sides of the arm. Splints should reach from the elbow to well beyond the wrist.

(3) Tie splints in place above and below the break.

(4) Support the lower arm with a wide sling tied around the neck. Sling should be placed so that the fingers are slightly higher (3 to 4 inches) than the level of the elbow.

(5) Victim is usually more comfortable sitting up while riding to the hospital.

(Illustration on page 87.)

Back

BEWARE
Never move a victim with a suspected back injury without trained medical assistance unless the victim is in immediate danger from fire, explosion or any other life-threatening situation. *Any* movement of the head, neck or back may result in paralysis or death.

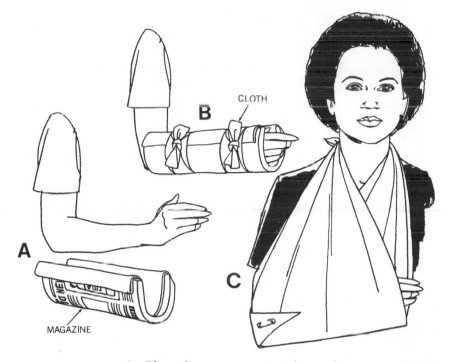

A. *Place lower arm at right angle across victim's chest with palm facing toward the chest and the thumb pointing upward. Apply padded splint on each side of his lower arm. Splint should reach from the elbow to beyond the wrist.*

B. *Tie splint in place above and below the break.*

C. *Support lower arm with a wide sling (see how to apply sling in Part I, page 40) tied around the neck. Fingers should be slightly higher (3 to 4 inches) than the level of the elbow.*

WHAT TO DO
(1) If the victim must be removed from an automobile, immobilize the back and neck with a short, reasonably wide board placed behind the victim's head, neck and back. The board should reach down to the victim's buttocks.

(2) Tie the board around the victim's forehead, under the armpits and around the lower abdomen, keeping those body parts on alignment with each other.

(3) *Do not* let the victim's body bend or twist. Move the victim very gently and slowly.

(4) If the victim is not breathing, tilt his head back slightly to maintain an open airway. If victim is face down, get adequate help so that every part of the body can be turned over together in the same position in which it was found. Restore breathing, if necessary.

(5) Summon paramedics or other trained ambulance personnel.

(6) Place folded blankets, towels or clothing at the victim's sides, head and neck to keep him from rotating or moving from side to side.

(7) Keep victim comfortably warm.

If victim with back injury must be taken to the hospital by someone *other* than trained medical personnel:

WHAT TO DO (1) If unsure whether injury is to the neck or back, treat as if there were a neck injury. (See Neck on pages 95–97.)

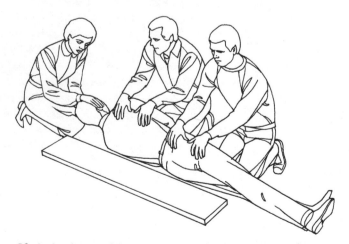

If victim is vomiting or unconscious, transport him on his side. Roll victim over as a unit, keeping victim's head in the same relationship to the body as it was found. Slide onto support as described above. Do not let head move. Move entire body together.

(2) Victim with a suspected broken back *must* be taken to the hospital lying down. If victim is conscious, transport in the position in which the victim was found; that is, face up or face down.

Do not, however, transport face down if victim has severe chest or face injuries. If victim is unconscious, transport him on his side to prevent choking on vomit. Roll victim over as a unit, keeping victim's head in the same relationship to the body as it was found.

(3) Place a well-padded rigid support such as a door, table leaf, wide board, etc., next to the victim.

(4) Slide ties under support.

(5) If victim is breathing on his own, hold his

(Continued on next page.)

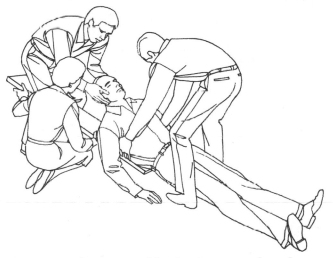

If victim with suspected back injury must be taken to the hospital by someone other than trained medical personnel, victim must be transported lying down. Place well-padded rigid support such as a door, etc., next to the victim. Victim's head must be held so that it stays in the same relationship to the body as it was found. Helpers should grasp victim's clothes and slide victim onto the support. Move entire body as a unit.

head so that it does not move but stays in the same relationship to the body as it was found. Other helpers should grasp victim's clothing and *slide* victim onto the support. Move the entire body together.

(6) *Do not lift* victim onto the support unless there is a minimum of four helpers, preferably six.

(7) Place folded towels, blankets or clothing at victim's sides, head and neck to keep him from moving. If victim is lying on his back, place padding in the hollow of his back.

(8) Tie or tape victim's body to the support.

(9) Drive carefully to prevent further injury.

Collar Bone

WHAT TO DO   With an elastic bandage or other cloth, apply a figure-of-eight bandage around the victim's shoulder, back and chest, as indicated by the illustration on this page.

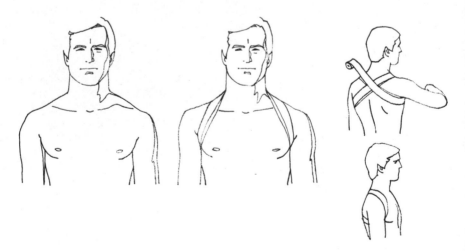

Wrap a bandage (starting under either arm) diagonally across the back, over the shoulder, under the arm and again diagonally across the back, and over the shoulder and under the arm, etc. Repeat a few more times. Illustration shows front, side and back views.

Elbow

Elbow fractures often cause circulatory problems. Victim should seek medical help at once if
an elbow injury is suspected.

If elbow is *bent:*

WHAT TO DO (1) *Do not* try to straighten the elbow.
(2) Place the forearm in a sling and tie around the
victim's neck if possible.
(3) If possible, bind the injured upper arm to the
victim's body by placing a towel, cloth, etc.,
around the upper arm, sling and chest and
tying it under victim's opposite arm.

If elbow is *straight:*

WHAT TO DO (1) *Do not* try to bend the elbow to apply a sling.
(2) Place padding in victim's armpit.
(3) Apply padded splints along one or both sides
of the entire arm. If splints are not available, a
pillow centered at the elbow and tied may be
used.

Foot

See Ankle on pages 84–85.

Hand

WHAT TO DO (1) Place a padded splint underneath the lower
arm and hand.
(2) Tie splint in place.
(3) Place the lower arm and the elbow at a right
angle to the victim's chest.
(4) Put the lower arm into a sling and tie around
the victim's neck.

(Illustration on next page.)

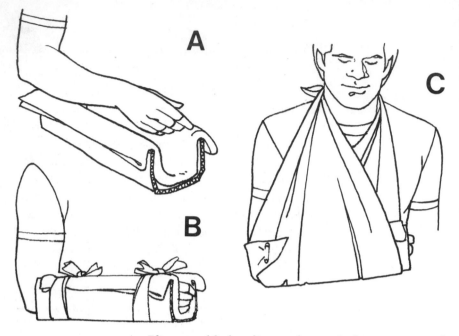

A. *Place padded splint underneath lower arm and hand.*
B. *Tie splint in place.*
C. *Place lower arm and elbow at right angle to victim's chest. Put lower arm into a sling and tie around victim's neck. (See how to apply sling in Part I, page 40.)*

Kneecap (**See also** Dislocations on page 130.)

WHAT TO DO
(1) Gently straighten victim's injured leg, if necessary.
(2) Place a padded board at least 4 inches wide underneath the injured leg. The board should be long enough to reach from the victim's heel to the buttocks.
(3) Place extra padding under the ankle and the knee.
(4) Tie the splint in place at the ankle, just below the knee, just above the knee and at the thigh. *Do not* tie over the kneecap.

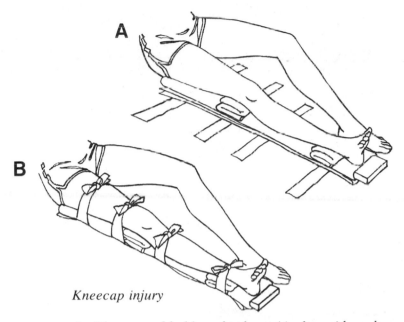

Kneecap injury

A. *Place a padded board at least 4 inches wide underneath injured leg. The board should reach from victim's heel to the buttocks. Place extra padding under the ankle and knee.*

B. *Tie splint in place at the ankle, just below and above the knee, and at the thigh.* Do not *tie over the kneecap.*

Upper Leg

If board splints are *not* available:

WHAT TO DO   (1) Carefully and slowly straighten the knee of the injured leg, if necessary.

(2) Place padding such as a folded blanket between the victim's legs.

(3) Tie the injured leg to the uninjured leg. Legs should be tied together in several places including around the ankles, above and below the knee and around the thigh.

Do *not* tie directly over the break.

(Continued on next page.)

If board splints are available:

WHAT TO DO   (1) Carefully and slowly straighten the knee of the injured leg if necessary.

(2) Assemble seven long bandages, cloth strips, etc. Use a stick or small board to push each strip under the victim's body at a hollow such as the ankle, knee or small of the back and then slide strip into place (ankle, above and below the knee, thigh, pelvis, lower back and just below the armpit).

(3) Place two well-padded splints in position. The outside splint should be long enough to reach from the victim's armpit to below the heel. The inside splint should reach from the crotch to below the heel.

(4) Tie the splints in place with knots at the outside splint.

Lower Leg

If splints are *not* available:

WHAT TO DO   (1) Carefully and slowly straighten the injured leg, if necessary.

(2) Place padding such as a folded blanket between the victim's legs.

(3) Tie legs together. (See Upper Leg.)

If splints are available:

WHAT TO DO   (1) Place a well-padded splint on each side of the injured leg. A third splint can be used underneath the leg. Splints should reach from above the knee to below the heel.

(2) Tie the splints together in three or four places. *Do not* tie directly over the break.

Pillow splint:

WHAT TO DO   (1) Gently lift the injured leg and slide the pillow under the leg.

(2) Bring the edges of the pillow to the top side of the leg. Pin the pillow together or tie the pillow around the leg in several places. For added support, place a rigid object such as a board or stick on each side of the pillow and fasten in place with ties above and below the suspected fracture site.

Neck

BEWARE

Never move a victim with a suspected neck injury without trained medical assistance unless the victim's life is in immediate danger from fire, explosion, etc. *Any* movement of the head, either forward, backward or side to side can result in paralysis or death.

WHAT TO DO
(1) If the victim must be moved because of immediate danger to his life, immobilize the neck with a rolled towel or newspaper about 4 inches wide wrapped around the neck and tied in place. (*Do not* allow the tie to interfere with victim's breathing.) If the victim is being rescued from an automobile, place a reasonably short, wide board behind the victim's head and back. Tie the board to the victim's body around the forehead and under the armpits. Move the victim very slowly and gently.
Do not let the victim's body bend or twist.
(2) If the victim is not breathing or is having great difficulty in breathing, tilt his head slightly backward to provide and maintain an open airway. Restore breathing if necessary by mouth-to-mouth resuscitation.
(3) Summon paramedics or trained ambulance personnel immediately.
(4) Lay folded towels, blankets, clothing, sandbags or other suitable objects around the victim's head, neck and shoulders to keep the head and neck from moving. Place bricks,

stones, etc., next to blankets for additional support.

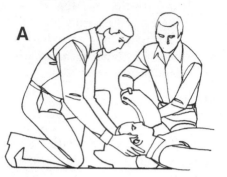

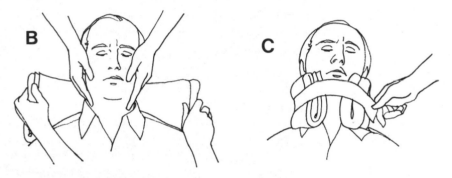

A. *If victim with suspected broken neck must be moved because of immediate danger to his life, immobilize neck with a rolled towel, etc., about 4 inches wide. Keep head as steady as possible.*
B. *Carefully wrap towel, etc., around victim's neck, keeping head as still as possible.*
C. *Tie wrap in place, being careful not to interfere with victim's breathing.*
D. *If victim is being rescued from an automobile, place a reasonably short, wide board behind victim's head and back. Tie board to victim's body around the forehead and under the armpits. Move victim slowly and gently.*

(5) Keep victim comfortably warm.

If victim must be taken to the hospital by someone *other* than trained medical personnel:

WHAT TO DO
(1) Victim must be transported lying down on his back, *face up* unless there is danger of vomiting in which case the victim's entire body, keeping the head in the same relationship to the body as it was found, must be rolled together on its side.
(2) Place a well-padded rigid support such as a door, table leaf, wide board, etc., next to the victim. Slide the ties under the support.
(3) If the victim is breathing on his own, hold his head so that it stays in the same relationship to the body as it was found. Other helpers should grasp the victim's clothes and *slide* the victim onto the support. Move the entire body together as a unit.
(4) *Do not lift* the victim onto the support unless there is a minimum of four helpers, preferably six.
(5) Place folded towels, blankets, cloths, etc., around the victim's head and neck to keep them from moving.
(6) Tie the victim's body to the support.
(7) Drive carefully to prevent further injury.

Pelvis

WHAT TO DO
(1) Keep the victim lying down on his back.
(2) Legs may be straight or bent at the knees, whichever is more comfortable for the victim.
(3) Tie the victim's legs together at the ankles and knees whether the legs are straight or bent.
(4) If the victim must be taken to the hospital by someone other than trained medical personnel, place victim on a well-padded rigid support such as a board, door, table leaf, etc. (See transporting back injury on pages 87–90.)

Shoulder

WHAT TO DO   (1) Place victim's injured forearm at a right angle to his chest.
(2) Apply a sling and tie around the victim's neck.
(3) Bind the arm to victim's body by placing a towel, cloth, etc., around upper arm and chest and tying under the victim's opposite arm.
(4) Victim is usually more comfortable sitting up while riding to the hospital.

Skull

After treating the skull injury, if blood is flowing from ear canal, see Ear Injuries on page 147.

WHAT TO DO   (1) Keep victim lying down and quiet.
(2) If victim's face is red and there is no evidence of neck or back injury (with a severe neck or back injury, victim may not be able to move arms, hands, fingers, and/or legs, feet, toes; victim may have tingling, numbness or pain in the neck or back), elevate the head and shoulders slightly with a pillow or a towel.
(3) If victim's face is pale, keep the head level with the rest of the body.
(4) If there is no evidence of a neck or back injury, turn victim's head to the side to allow secretions to drain.
(5) Control any bleeding from the scalp by applying direct pressure.
(6) Keep victim comfortably warm.
(7) *Do not* give the victim anything by mouth.
(8) Seek medical attention promptly.
(9) If ambulance is unavailable, take the victim to the hospital lying down. Place pads or other suitable objects on each side of victim's head to keep it from moving.
See Also: Bleeding; Dislocations; Head Injuries; Shock; Sprains; Wounds

● **Bug bites:** see Bites and Stings
● **Bullet wounds:** see Wounds (puncture wounds)

BRUISES

A bruise is the most common type of injury. It occurs when a fall or blow to the body causes small blood vessels to break beneath the skin. The discoloration and swelling in the skin is caused by the blood seeping into the tissues which change colors as the bruise heals.

SYMPTOMS
(1) Pain.
(2) Initial reddening of the skin.
(3) Later, the bruise turns blue or green in color.
(4) Occasionally, a lump called a hematoma forms at the site.
(5) Finally, the area becomes brown and yellow before fading away.

WHAT TO DO
(1) As soon as possible apply cold compresses or an ice bag to the affected area to decrease local bleeding and swelling.
(2) If bruise is on the arm or leg, elevate the limb above the level of the heart to decrease local blood flow.
(3) After 24 hours, apply moist heat (a warm wet compress) to aid healing.
(4) If bruise is severe or painful swelling develops, seek medical attention as there is the possibility of a broken bone or other injury.
See Also: Bleeding; Broken Bones and Spinal Injuries; Dislocations; Lumps and Bumps; Muscle Aches and Pains

BURNS

ABCs

With all serious injuries, check and maintain an open Airway. Restore Breathing and Circulation if necessary.

Tilt head backward to maintain an open airway.

The objectives of first aid for burns are to relieve pain, prevent infection and prevent or treat for shock.

Burns caused by *fire, sunlight* or *hot substances* are classified according to the degree of the injury—first-degree burns being the least dangerous, third-degree burns the most.

FIRST-DEGREE BURNS

A burn resulting in injury only to the outside layer of the skin is a first-degree burn. Sunburn, brief contact with hot objects, hot water or steam are common causes of first-degree burns and cause no blistering of the burned areas.

SYMPTOMS

(1) Redness.
(2) Mild swelling.
(3) Pain.
(4) Unbroken skin (no blisters).
(5) Any one or all of the above may be present.

WHAT TO DO

(1) Immediately put burned area under cold running water or apply cold-water compress

(clean towel, washcloth, handkerchief, etc.) until pain decreases.

(2) Cover burn with sterile or clean bandages.

Do not apply butter or grease to a burn. Do not apply other medications or home remedies without a doctor's recommendation.

Immediately put burned area under cold running water (as illustrated) or apply cold-water compresses until pain subsides.

SECOND-DEGREE BURNS

A burn that causes injury to the layers of skin beneath the surface of the body is a second-degree burn. Deep sunburn, hot liquids and flash burns from gasoline and other substances are common causes of second-degree burns.

SYMPTOMS

(1) Redness, or blotchy or streaking appearance to burn.
(2) Blisters.
(3) Swelling that lasts for several days.
(4) Moist, oozy appearance to the surface of the skin.
(5) Pain.
(6) Any one or all of the above may be present.

WHAT TO DO

(1) Put burned area in cold water (not iced) or apply cold-water compresses (clean towel,

washcloth, handkerchief, etc.) until pain subsides.

(2) Gently pat the area dry with a clean towel or other soft material.

(3) Cover burned area with a dry sterile bandage or clean cloth to prevent infection.

(4) Elevate burned arms or legs.

(5) Seek medical attention. If victim has flash burns around the lips or nose, or has singed nasal hairs, breathing problems may develop. Seek medical attention immediately, preferably at the nearest hospital emergency room.

Do not attempt to break blisters.

Do not apply ointments, sprays, antiseptics or home remedies.

BEWARE

Prompt medical attention is required for burns that cover over 15 percent of the body of an adult or 10 percent of the body of a child, or for burns of the face, hands or feet. To determine the percentage of burned area, an easy rule is that your hand (including fingers) represents 1 percent of your body area. Victims who have inhaled smoke or other substances can develop lung damage.

THIRD-DEGREE BURNS

A burn that destroys all layers of the skin is a third-degree burn. Fire and prolonged contact with hot substances or electrical burns are common causes of third-degree burns.

SYMPTOMS

(1) Burned area appears white or charred.

(2) Destroyed skin.

(3) Little pain is present because nerve endings have been destroyed.

(4) Any one or all of the above may be present.

BEWARE

(1) *Do not* remove clothes that are stuck to the burn.

(2) *Do not* put ice or ice water on burns. This can intensify shock reaction.

(3) *Do not* apply ointments, sprays, antiseptics or home remedies to burns.

IMMEDIATE TREATMENT

(1) If victim is on fire, smother flames with blanket, bedspread, rug, etc.

(2) Breathing difficulties are frequent with burns, particularly with burns around the face, neck and mouth, and with smoke inhalation. Check to be sure that the victim is breathing.

(3) Place cold cloth or cool water (not iced) on burns of the face, hands or feet to cool the burned areas.

(4) Cover burned area with thick sterile dressings. A clean sheet, pillow case, disposable diaper, etc., can be used.

(5) Call for an ambulance immediately. It is very important that victims with even *small* third-degree burns consult a doctor.

CONTINUED CARE

(1) Elevate burned hands higher than the victim's heart, if possible.

(2) Elevate burned legs or feet. Do not allow victim to walk.

(3) If victim has face or neck burns, he should be propped up with pillows. Check often to see if victim has trouble breathing and maintain an open airway if breathing becomes difficult.

(4) Treat for shock.

    (a) Keep victim lying down unless face or neck is burned.

    (b) Elevate victim's feet 8 to 12 inches unless the victim is unconscious, has neck, spine, head, chest or severe lower face or jaw injuries. A victim who is unconscious or who has severe lower face or jaw injuries should be placed on his side (not face down) with his head slightly extended to prevent choking on fluids or

vomit. If victim is having trouble breathing, elevate his head and shoulders
slightly.

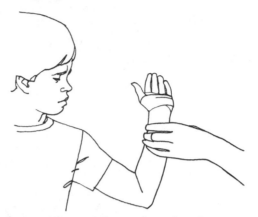

*Cover burn with a sterile or clean bandage to prevent
infection. Elevate a second- or third-degree burned
hand or arm higher than the victim's heart.*

(c) If pain increases, lower feet again.
(d) Keep victim comfortably warm with a
blanket or coat, etc., but not hot. If possible, place a blanket beneath a victim who
is on the ground.

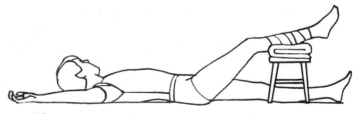

*Elevate a second- or third-degree burned foot or leg
higher than the victim's heart.*

(e) If medical attention is more than two
hours away, give the victim water or a
weak solution of salt (1 level teaspoon),
baking soda (one-half level teaspoon),
mixed with 1 quart cool water. Give an
adult 4 ounces (one-half glass); a child 1

through 12 years old, 2 ounces; and an infant 1 ounce. Have victim sip slowly over a 15-minute period and repeat every 15 minutes. Clear juices, such as apple juice, may also be given.

Do not give fluid if victim is unconscious, having convulsions, is likely to need surgery, has a brain injury or an abdominal wound, or is vomiting. Stop giving fluids if vomiting occurs.

(f) *Do not* give victim alcohol.

(g) Calm and reassure victim. Gentleness, kindness and understanding play an important role in treating a victim in shock.

CHEMICAL BURNS

IMMEDIATE TREATMENT

(1) Quickly flush burned area with large quantities of running water over the affected area for at least five minutes. Speed and plenty of water are both important in minimizing the extent of the injury. Use a garden hose, buckets of water, a shower or tub. Do not use a strong stream of water if it can be avoided.

(2) Continue to flush with water while removing clothing from burned area.

(*Continued on next page.*)

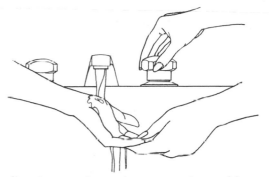

Immediately put burned area under cold running water (as illustrated) or apply cold-water compresses until pain subsides.

(3) After flushing, follow instructions on label of chemical causing burn, if available.

(4) Cover burn with clean bandage or clean cloth.

(5) Seek medical attention, but treat first as directed above. *Do not* apply ointments, sprays, antiseptics or home remedies. Cool wet dressings are best for pain.

See Also: Part I, pages 31–32; Convulsions; Electric Shock; Overexposure: Heat and Cold; Shock

● **Cardiopulmonary resuscitation (CPR):** see Part I, page 11

● **Cavities:** see Dental Emergencies

● **Charley horse:** see Muscle Aches and Pains

● **Chemical burns:** see Burns (chemical burns); Eye Injuries (burns, chemical)

● **Chemical inhalation:** see Poisons (poisoning from smoke, chemical or gas fumes)

● **Chest pain:** see Heart Attack; Shock

● **Chest wounds:** see Wounds (chest wounds)

● **Chicken pox:** see Rashes (diseases)

CHILDBIRTH, EMERGENCY

Occasionally childbirth occurs at an unexpected time or labor proceeds more quickly than expected. In such cases, the mother sometimes cannot get to the hospital in time for the delivery of the infant.

If the mother's contractions are two to three minutes apart, if she feels the urge to push down or to move her bowels, or if the baby's head is visible (about the size of a half-dollar or larger) in the vaginal opening, birth will usually occur very soon.

If at all possible, summon a doctor to deliver

the infant. Sometimes a doctor can give instructions over the telephone during the delivery.

Try to remain calm. Most births occur naturally and normally.

Do not try to delay or prevent the birth of the baby by crossing the mother's legs or pushing on the baby's head or by any other means. This could be very harmful to the infant.

PREPARATION FOR DELIVERY

Before the Baby Arrives

WHAT TO DO

(1) Place clean sheets on the bed. If time allows, a shower curtain or rubber sheet placed underneath the clean linen will help protect the mattress. If no bed is readily available, place clean cloths, clothes or newspapers underneath the mother's hips and thighs on the floor or ground. A fresh newspaper is generally very clean and almost sterile.

(2) Have the mother lie on her back with her knees bent, feet flat and her knees and thighs wide apart. If the mother is on a bed, leave enough room for the birth of the baby.

(3) Wash your hands with soap and water.

(*Continued on next page.*)

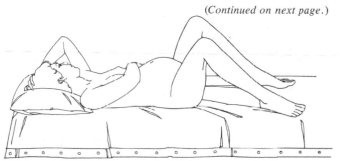

Place clean sheets on the bed. If no bed is available, place clean cloths, clothes or newspapers underneath the mother's hips and thighs on the floor. Leaving room for the birth of the baby, have the mother lie on her back with her knees bent, feet flat and her knees and thighs wide apart.

(4) Sterilize scissors or knife in boiling water for at least five minutes if possible or hold over a flame for 30 seconds. Leave the scissors in the water until you are ready to use them. The scissors may be used to cut the umbilical cord.

(5) Gather together:

(a) A clean, soft cotton blanket, sheet or towel to wrap the baby in after it is born.

(b) Clean, strong string, white shoelaces, cord or strips of cloth to be used to tie off the umbilical cord.

(c) A pail or bucket to be used if the mother vomits.

(d) A large plastic bag, container or towel in which to place the afterbirth (placenta) for later inspection by medical personnel.

(e) Sanitary napkins or clean folded cloths or handkerchiefs to be placed over the vagina after the birth of the baby and the delivery of the afterbirth.

(f) Diapers and safety pins.

Delivering the Baby

WHAT TO DO
(1) *Do not* place your hands or other objects in the vagina.

(2) *Do not* interfere with the delivery or touch the baby until the head is completely out of the vagina.

(3) Once the baby's head is out, guide and support it to keep it free of blood and other secretions.

(4) If the baby's head is still inside a liquid-filled bag, *carefully* puncture the bag to allow the fluid to escape and remove the membranes from baby's face so that the baby can breathe.

(5) Usually the baby's head will be born face down. Check to make sure the umbilical cord is not wrapped around the baby's neck. If it is, gently and quickly slip the cord over the baby's head.

(6) If the cord is wrapped too tightly to slip over the baby's head, the cord must be cut now to prevent the baby from choking. This is a *rare occurrence*, however. Squeeze *both* cut ends tightly with a cloth or your fingers until they can be properly tied. (See Immediate Care of the Baby, number 8, now, on page 111.)

(7) Continue to support the head as the baby is being born. The baby will be very slippery so be gentle and very careful.

(8) Once the baby's head and neck are out of the vagina, the baby will turn himself on his side (facing his mother's thighs) to allow for the birth of his shoulders. The upper shoulder usually passes first. *Carefully* and *gently* guide the baby's head slightly downward. Once the upper shoulder is out, *gently* lift the baby's head upward to allow the lower shoulder to emerge.

(9) Carefully hold the slippery baby as the rest of his body slides out.

Immediate Care of the Baby

WHAT TO DO

(1) To help the baby start breathing, hold the baby with his head lower than his feet so that secretions can drain from his lungs, mouth and nose. Support the head and body with one hand while grasping the baby's legs at the ankles with the other hand.

(2) Wipe out the mouth and nose gently with sterile gauze or a clean cloth to make sure that nothing hampers breathing.

(3) If the baby has not yet cried, slap your fingers against the bottom of the baby's feet or gently rub the baby's back.

(4) If the baby is still not breathing, give artificial respiration through *both* the baby's mouth and nose, keeping the head extended. Give very gentle puffs every three seconds.

(5) Note the time of delivery.

After the baby is born, hold the baby with his head lower than his feet so that secretions can drain from his lungs, mouth and nose. Support the head and body with one hand while grasping the baby's legs and ankles with the other hand.

(6) Once the baby starts breathing, wrap the infant, including the top and back of his head, in a blanket or sheet, etc. Place the baby on his side on the mother's stomach with the baby's head slightly lower than the rest of his body. The baby should be facing his mother's feet. The umbilical cord should be kept slack. It is very important that the baby be kept warm and breathing well.

Do not clean the white cheesy coating covering the baby's skin. This is a protective covering. *Do not* clean the baby's eyes, ears or nose.

(7) It is not necessary or desirable to cut the umbilical cord immediately. It is best to wait about five minutes until the cord stops pulsating. If the mother can be taken to the hos-

pital immediately after the delivery of the afterbirth (placenta), the baby can be left attached to the umbilical cord and afterbirth, particularly if there are no clean scissors, etc., to cut the cord. Also, the cord must be cut properly.

(8) If you must cut the cord, tie a clean string, strip of cloth, etc., around the cord at least 4 inches from the baby's body. Tie the string in a tight square knot so that circulation is cut off in the cord. Using a second piece of string, etc., tie another *tight* square knot 6 to 8 inches from the baby (2 to 4 inches from the first knot) toward the mother.

(9) Cut the cord *between* the two ties with sterilized or clean scissors or knife.

(Continued on next page.)

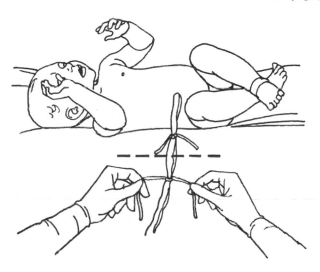

If the umbilical cord is to be cut (see Immediate Care of the Baby number 7 in the text), tie a clean string around the cord at least 4 inches from the baby's body. Tie in a tight square knot so that circulation is cut off in the cord. Use a second piece of string to tie another tight *square knot 6 to 8 inches from the baby (2 to 4 inches from the first knot) toward the mother. Cut the cord* between *the two ties.*

(10) Keep the baby warm with his head also covered and close to his mother. The baby's head should still be slightly lower than the rest of his body to allow for drainage of secretions.

DELIVERY OF THE AFTERBIRTH

Delivery of the afterbirth (placenta) usually occurs within 5 to 20 minutes after the birth of the baby. It is usually preceded by a gush of dark red blood from the vagina.

WHAT TO DO
(1) Be patient in waiting for the delivery of the afterbirth.
(2) *Do not* pull on the umbilical cord to quicken delivery of the afterbirth. The mother's uterine contractions will eventually push out the afterbirth.
(3) There will be bleeding with the birth of the baby and the afterbirth.
(4) Place the afterbirth in a container and take it with the mother and the baby to the hospital (preferably) or other medical facility so that it may be examined.

CARE OF THE MOTHER

After the infant has been born:

(1) Place sanitary napkins or other clean folded cloths against the mother's vaginal opening to absorb blood.
(2) To help control the flow of blood from the mother, place your hands on the mother's abdomen and gently massage the uterus, which can be felt just below the mother's navel and feels like a large smooth ball. Continue to massage gently until the uterus feels *firm*.

Continue to do this every five minutes or so
for an hour, unless medical assistance is obtained sooner. If the bleeding is very heavy
and/or prolonged, seek medical attention immediately.
(3) Sponge the mother's face with cool water if
she wishes.
(4) Give the mother tea, coffee, broth, etc., if she
desires something to drink. *Do not* give her alcoholic beverages.
(5) Keep the mother warm and comfortable. And
remember, congratulations are in order!

MEDICAL ATTENTION

Regardless of how smoothly the delivery goes, it
is very important that both the mother and the
baby be examined by a physician to make certain
all is well. Most serious problems occur in the
first 24 hours after birth.
See Also: Miscarriage; Pregnancy, Danger Signs

CHILLS

Chills may be a symptom for flu, kidney and bladder infections, bacterial pneumonia, salmonella
food poisoning, brown recluse spider bites or
many other medical problems.
Chills are also associated with exposure to
cold. (See Overexposure: Heat and Cold.)
Chills are nature's way of raising the body temperature. Chills occur when there is decreased
blood circulation to the body surface due to narrowing of the blood vessels in the skin. Muscles in
the body also contract. Shivering and shaking associated with chills produce heat in the body, thus
allowing the body temperature to rise. Often,
chills are followed by fever and indicate the onset
of an infectious process.

Make the victim comfortably warm. Do not use hot water bottles or heating pads. Warm drinks and liquids such as tea or soup are also helpful if the victim is not nauseated or vomiting. It is advisable to seek medical attention as a serious infection may be present.

See Also: Bites and Stings (spider bites); Fever; Overexposure: Heat and Cold; Poisons (food)

CHOKING

SYMPTOMS
(1) Gasping or noisy breathing.
(2) Victim grasps his throat.
(3) Inability to talk.
(4) Difficulty in breathing. Coughing. Breathing may stop.
(5) Skin becomes pale, white, gray or blue.
(6) Panic in expression and action.
(7) Unconsciousness eventually develops.

If victim is standing or sitting, stand behind and slightly to one side of him and support his chest with one hand. With the heel of the other hand give four quick, very forceful blows on the back between the victim's shoulder blades.

If the victim is *conscious:*
(If victim is unconscious, see pages 117–18.)

IMMEDIATE TREATMENT

(1) If the victim can speak, cough or breathe, *do not* interfere in any way with the victim's efforts to cough out a swallowed or partially swallowed object.

(2) If the victim cannot breathe and is standing or sitting, stand behind and slightly to one side of him and support his chest with one hand. With the heel of the other hand give *four* quick, very forceful blows on the back between the victim's shoulder blades.

(3) If the victim is lying down, kneel beside the victim and roll him onto his side so that he is facing you. Place the victim's chest against your knees for support. With the heel of your hand give *four* quick, very forceful blows on the victim's back between the shoulder blades.

(Continued on next page.)

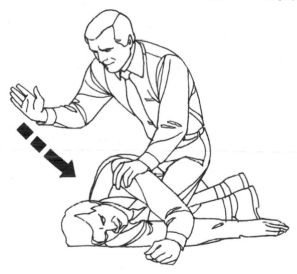

If victim is lying down, kneel beside victim and roll him onto his side so that he is facing you. Place victim's chest against your knee. With the heel of your hand give four quick, very forceful blows on the victim's back between the shoulder blades.

(4) If the above procedures do not dislodge the object and the victim is standing or sitting, stand behind the victim with your arms around his waist. Place your fist with the thumb side against the victim's stomach slightly above the navel and below the ribs and breastbone. Hold your fist with your other hand and give *four* quick, forceful upward thrusts. This maneuver increases pressure in the abdomen which pushes up the diaphragm. This in turn increases the air pressure in the lungs and will hopefully force out the object. Do not squeeze with your arms, just use your fists.

(5) If the victim is lying down, turn him on his back. Kneel beside the victim and put the heel

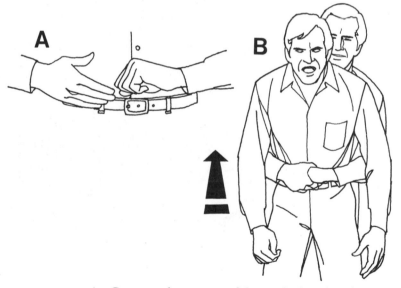

A. *Correct placement of fist with thumb side against victim's stomach slightly above the navel and below the ribs and breastbone.*

B. *If victim is standing or sitting, stand behind victim with your arms around his waist. Place your fist as shown in illustration. Hold your fist with your other hand and give four quick, forceful upward thrusts.*

of one hand on the victim's stomach slightly above the navel and below the ribs. Keep your elbows straight. Put your free hand on top of the other to provide additional force. Give *four* quick, very forceful upward and backward thrusts in an attempt to dislodge the object.

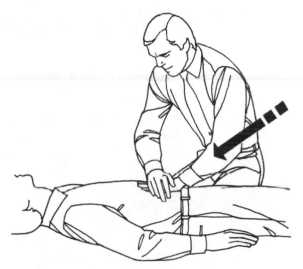

If victim is lying down, turn him on his back. Kneel beside the victim and put the heel of one hand on the victim's stomach slightly above the navel and below the ribs. Keep elbows straight. Put your free hand on top of the fist. Give four quick, very forceful downward and forward thrusts toward the head.

(6) If this gives no results, repeat the back blows and the upward abdominal thrusts until the victim coughs up the object or becomes unconscious. Look to see if the object appears in the victim's mouth or top of his throat. Use your fingers to pull it out.

(Continued on next page.)

If the victim is *unconscious* or *becomes unconscious:*

IMMEDIATE
TREATMENT

(1) Place the victim on his back on a rigid surface.

(2) Open the victim's airway by extending the head back. Try to restore breathing with mouth-to-mouth respiration. (See Electric Shock, Immediate Treatment, pages 151–55.)

(3) If still unsuccessful, turn the victim on his side and give *four* quick, very forceful blows on his back between the shoulder blades. (See page 115, Immediate Treatment, number 3, for conscious victim lying down.)

(4) If still unsuccessful, turn the victim on his back and give *four* quick, forceful upward abdominal thrusts. (See pages 116–17, Immediate Treatment, number 5, for conscious victim lying down.)

(5) If these procedures fail, grab the victim's lower jaw and tongue with one hand and lift up to remove the tongue from the back of the throat. Place the index finger of the other hand inside the victim's mouth alongside the cheek. Slide your fingers down into the throat to the base of the victim's tongue.

Carefully sweep your fingers along the back of the throat to dislodge the object. Bring your fingers out along the inside of the other cheek. Be careful not to push the object further down the victim's throat.

Do not attempt to remove the foreign object with any type of instrument or forceps.

(6) Repeat all of the above steps until the object is dislodged or medical assistance arrives. Do not give up!

(7) Seek medical assistance for all choking victims even if the object is dislodged and breathing is restored because respiratory tract damage or other problems may occur.

If the victim is an *infant* or a *small child:*

IMMEDIATE TREATMENT

(1) Place the infant or small child across your forearm or lap with his head low and his face down.

(2) Give *four* quick blows with the heel of your hand on the child's back between his shoulder blades. Blows should be gentler than those used on an adult.

(3) If unsuccessful, turn child over onto his back and give *four* quick abdominal thrusts. Thrusts should be gentler than those used on an adult. (See pages 116–17), Immediate Treatment, number 5, for conscious victim lying down.)

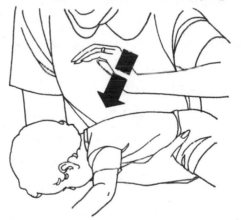

Place infant or small child across your forearm or lap with his head low and his face down. Give four quick blows on the child's back between his shoulder blades. Blows should be more gentle than those for an adult. (See text for abdominal thrusts if this procedure does not work.)

If the victim is very *fat* or is *pregnant:*

IMMEDIATE TREATMENT

(1) Apply *four* quick back blows as described earlier.

(2) Place your fist and your other hand up the middle of the breastbone in the chest (not

over the ribs) and give *four* quick, forceful thrust movements. *Do not* squeeze with your arms—use your fists.

If you are *alone* and choking:

IMMEDIATE TREATMENT

(1) Place your fist and other hand into your stomach slightly above your navel and below your ribs. Give yourself *four* quick, forceful upward abdominal thrusts.
(2) Pressing your stomach forcefully over a chair, table, sink, railing, etc., may also be helpful.
See Also: Part I, pages 16–20; Unconscious

Circulation restoration: see Part I, pages 14 – 15; Drowning; Electric Shock; Heart Attack; Unconscious

Codeine, abuse: see Drug Abuse

Colds: see Chills

Cold sweat: see Chills

Cold water drowning: see Drowning

Coma: see Drug Abuse; Unconscious

Conjunctivitis: see Eye Injuries (pink eye)

Constipation: see Abdominal Pain

Contact lenses: see Eye Injuries (contact lenses)

Contaminated food: see Poisons (food poisoning)

Contractions: see Childbirth, Emergency

CONVULSIONS (SEIZURES)

Convulsions are a series of uncontrollable muscle movements during a state of total or partial unconsciousness. There may be a temporary loss of breathing. A convulsion (seizure) results from a disturbance in electrical activity in the brain. Most convulsions last less than a few minutes.

Convulsions may occur with a head injury, brain tumor, epilepsy (see Epileptic Seizures on pages 122–23), poisoning, electric shock, withdrawal from drugs, heat stroke, scorpion bites, poisonous snake bites, hyperventilation or high fever (particularly in young children—see Convulsions in Infants and Children on pages 123–24).

Although convulsions *appear* alarming, they rarely cause serious problems in themselves. Injuries may result from falling during the seizure or from surrounding objects.

SYMPTOMS

(1) Victim utters short cry or scream.
(2) Rigid muscles followed by jerky, twitching movements.
(3) Breathing may stop temporarily during seizure.
(4) Bluish color to the face and lips.
(5) Eyes may roll upward.
(6) Possible loss of bladder and bowel control.
(7) Drooling or foaming (may be bloody) at the mouth.
(8) Sleepiness and confusion after the convulsion is over.
(9) Unresponsiveness during seizure.
(10) Any one or all of the above may be present.

WHAT TO DO

(1) If victim starts to fall, try to catch him and lay him down gently.
(2) Remove any surrounding objects that the victim might strike during the convulsion or remove victim from dangerous surroundings (such as stairs, glass doors, fireplace, etc.).
(3) If breathing stops and does not start again momentarily after the seizure, maintain an open airway. Check to make sure victim's tongue is not blocking his throat. Restore breathing if necessary after the seizure.
(4) *Do not* interfere with convulsive movements, but be sure that victim does not injure him-

self. *Don't* try to hold victim down as muscle tears or fractures may result.

(5) *Do not* force any object such as a spoon or pencil between the victim's teeth.

(6) *Do not* throw any liquid on the victim's face or into his mouth.

(7) Loosen tight clothing around victim's neck and waist.

(8) After the convulsion is over, turn the victim's head to the side or place victim on his side to prevent choking on secretions, blood or vomit.

(9) Keep victim lying down after convulsion is over as he may be confused for a while.

(10) If necessary, shield victim from crowd to prevent embarrassment.

(11) Check for other injuries such as bleeding and broken bones and administer appropriate treatment.

(12) Stay with victim while he recovers.

(13) Seek medical attention promptly, particularly if seizure is followed by a second convulsion or if the victim is pregnant.

EPILEPTIC SEIZURE

Epilepsy is a disorder in which the victim has a hereditary tendency to have convulsions. It results when certain brain cells temporarily become overactive and release too much electrical energy. Sometimes the victim has a warning sensation (aura) that a seizure is about to occur and often utters a short scream or cry just before the attack. Symptoms during the seizure are the same as those for convulsions on page 121.

WHAT TO DO The treatment for a known epileptic seizure is the same as for convulsions (see pages 121–22). The primary aim is to prevent the victim from harming himself. *Do not* interfere with the convulsive movements. After the seizure, maintain an open airway and restore breathing if the victim should cease breathing and not start again momentarily. When the seizure is over, allow the victim to rest or sleep. It is always best to consult the victim's doctor. Always seek immediate medical attention if the seizure lasts longer than five minutes, if another convulsion follows the first, or if the victim is pregnant.

CONVULSIONS IN INFANTS AND CHILDREN

Convulsions in young children are not uncommon. The most frequent cause is a rapid rise in temperature due to an acute infection.

These convulsions are called febrile convulsions and occur usually in a child between 1 and 4 years of age. Febrile convulsions seldom last longer than two to three minutes. Although all convulsions in young children must be taken seriously, they are usually more frightening to watch than dangerous. The symptoms for febrile convulsions are the same as for convulsions on page 121.

WHAT TO DO

(1) Do not panic.
(2) Maintain an open airway. Check to make sure that the child's tongue is not blocking his throat.
(3) After the seizure, turn the child's head to one side or place the child on his side so that he will not choke if he should vomit.
(4) Remove the child's clothes and sponge his body with lukewarm water to help reduce his fever.
(5) *Do not* place the child in a tub of water as he may inhale the water during the convulsion.
(6) *Do not* throw water on the child's face or into his mouth.

(7) Have someone else call the child's doctor during the convulsion if you do not want to leave the child unattended. If this is impossible, call the doctor when the convulsion is over. If the doctor is not available, take the child to the hospital.

See Also: Part I, page 33; Drug Abuse; Fever; Headaches; Head Injuries; Overexposure: Heat and Cold; Poisons; Pregnancy, Danger Signs; Shock

Copperhead snake bites: see Bites and Stings (snakes)

Coral snake bites: see Bites and Stings (snakes)

Coronary: see Heart Attack

Cottonmouth snake bites: see Bites and Stings (snakes)

Coughing: see Asthma; Choking; Croup

CPR (Cardiopulmonary resuscitation): see Part I, page 11

Cramps: see Abdominal Pain; Diarrhea; Miscarriage; Muscle Aches and Pains; Overexposure: Heat and Cold (heat injuries); Pregnancy, Danger Signs

CROUP

Croup is not a disease. It is a group of symptoms arising from various respiratory conditions in children. Croup is generally caused by an allergy, or by a viral or bacterial infection.

SYMPTOMS

(1) Difficulty in breathing, particularly inhaling.
(2) Hoarseness.
(3) Hacking, barklike cough.
(4) Croaking sound upon inhaling (called "stridor" by your doctor).
(5) Possible slight fever.
(6) Possible bluish tinge to skin and lips.
(7) Victim is very restless.
(8) Any one or all of the above may be present.

WHAT TO DO It is important to remain calm during an attack of croup. Reassure the child so that he does not become overly frightened. *Do not* place a spoon or other object in the victim's mouth to aid breathing as this may cause airway obstruction. If the child has no fever, can be reasonably calmed, and if his skin and lips are not blue, take him into the bathroom and close the door. Turn on the hot water in the tub or shower to create steam. This makes breathing easier. Hold the child in a sitting position. *Do not* put the child in the water. A small child can be held up high where the steam accumulates. Remain in the bathroom for 20 to 30 minutes.

A cool-mist vaporizer is very helpful and should be placed in the child's room.

DANGER SIGNALS If symptoms continue and one or more of the following happen:

(1) Condition worsens after the child has been awake a short while.
(2) Extreme difficulty in breathing.
(3) Croaking sound while inhaling continues when child is calm (called "stridor" by your doctor).
(4) Skin and lips are blue.
(5) Sudden moderate or high fever.
(6) Child is exhausted and incapacitated.
(7) Drooling.

Then:

Seek medical attention promptly. Call a paramedic unit if one is available or go to the nearest hospital emergency room.

Croup is a condition occurring in infants and young children but is occasionally seen in the older child. It is most common during the cool months of the year. Most attacks of croup occur at night after the child has gone to bed. Often the child has had a mild cold before the attack of croup. Croup that occurs during the day generally becomes more severe in the evening.

- **Cuts:** see Bleeding; Eye Injuries (cuts); Head Injuries; Wounds (cuts)
- **Deafness:** see Ear Injuries and Earaches
- **Delerium tremens:** see Drug Abuse
- **Delivery:** see Childbirth, Emergency

DENTAL EMERGENCIES

TOOTHACHE

Cavities and infections often cause toothaches. Home treatment offers only temporary relief from pain but is often helpful if a toothache occurs in the middle of the night or before seeking professional attention. Dental attention is necessary to find the exact cause of a toothache and to treat it effectively.

WHAT TO DO
(1) Give victim aspirin or other similar medication. Aspirin should be swallowed and *not* applied directly to the affected area.
(2) Place cold compresses or ice packs on the face over the affected area. For some victims, warm compresses may be more comforting. This varies for each individual.
(3) Seek dental attention.

PULLED TOOTH (Extraction)

Pain, slight swelling and bleeding often occur after a tooth has been pulled. If these problems become severe or persistent, consult your dentist.

WHAT TO DO
(1) As soon as possible after the tooth has been pulled, place a cold compress or ice bag on the

face in the affected area to relieve swelling. It should remain in place for 15 minutes out of each hour. Repeat procedure for several hours.

(2) If bleeding is present:

    (a) Place a tea bag in boiling water for five to ten minutes. Remove and allow to cool. Rinse mouth with warm salt water. Place tea bag on bleeding area and close teeth tightly so that firm pressure is applied. Tea contains tannic acid which helps blood vessels to clot and stop bleeding.

    (b) If no tea bag is available, fold a clean piece of gauze, handkerchief or tissue into a pad and place over the wound. Close teeth tightly so that firm pressure can be applied against the bleeding area. Maintain pressure for 20 to 30 minutes. Repeat procedure if necessary.

(3) If dentist did not prescribe medication for pain, aspirin may be taken. Aspirin should be swallowed, *not* placed directly over the wound.

KNOCKED-OUT TEETH

WHAT TO DO
(1) Treat for bleeding. See Pulled Tooth on pages 126–27.

(2) Wrap the tooth in a cool wet cloth and take the victim and the tooth to the dentist as soon as possible.

See Also: Head Injuries

● **Depressants, abuse:** see Drug Abuse

● **Depression:** see Drug Abuse; Suicide, Threatened

● **Diabetic coma:** see Part I, page 20; Unconscious (diabetic coma)

● **Diaper rash:** see Rashes (rashes in infants)

DIARRHEA

Diarrhea is frequent elimination of loose, watery stools.

ADULTS

SYMPTOMS
(1) Frequent loose and watery stools. Stools may vary in color from light tan to green.
(2) Stomach cramping.
(3) Tiredness.
(4) Thirst.
(5) Any one or all of the above may be present.

WHAT TO DO
(1) A clear liquid diet is recommended to replace lost fluids. (Water, tea, carbonated beverages [shake up to eliminate fizz], Jello® or Jello® water, Kool-Aid®, clear broth, etc.)
(2) If diarrhea persists longer than a day or two, seek medical attention because fatal dehydration may occur.
(3) *Avoid* solid foods.

If symptoms continue and either or both of the following happen:

(1) Bloody stools or stools that are black in color.
(2) Severe or prolonged stomach cramping.

Then:

Seek prompt medical attention by your doctor or hospital emergency room.

There are many causes of diarrhea. Among the most common are food poisoning, mushroom poisoning, dysentery, certain medications, emotional stress, excessive drinking of alcoholic beverages, viral and bacterial infections, and stomach flu (viral gastroenteritis).

INFANTS AND CHILDREN

SYMPTOMS Frequent elimination of loose, watery stools. (Stools may or may not have a bad odor.)

WHAT TO DO (1) A clear liquid diet is recommended (water, tea, carbonated beverages [shake up to eliminate fizz], Jello® or Jello® water, Kool-Aid®).
(2) *Avoid* solid foods.

DANGER SIGNALS Diarrhea in infants can rapidly lead to severe dehydration or indicate other serious problems. Signs to look for are:

(1) Three or four loose, watery stools.
(2) Fever.
(3) Dry mouth.
(4) Failure to urinate.
(5) Drowsy, sluggish, weak cry.
(6) Sunken eyes.
(7) Vomiting.
(8) Blood in stools.

If these danger signals occur, seek medical attention promptly.

Common causes of diarrhea in infants and children are infection, spoiled food, food allergies, foods with laxative effects and poisoning.
Note:

If diarrhea is not severe and the child will take liquids, the body is making an effort to replace lost fluids. If the child or adult won't take liquids or is vomiting, replacement of fluids will be impossible and dehydration can occur rapidly, especially in children and infants. Hospitalization may be necessary.

See Also: Abdominal Pain; Poisons (food); Vomiting

DISLOCATIONS

A dislocation occurs when the end of a bone is displaced from its joint. It usually results from a fall or a blow to the bone. Common areas of dislocations include the shoulder, hip, elbow, fingers, thumb and kneecap.

SYMPTOMS
(1) Swelling.
(2) Deformity at the joint.
(3) Pain upon moving the injured part or inability to move the part.
(4) Discoloration of the skin around the area of the injury.
(5) Tenderness upon touching the area.
(6) Any one or all of the above may be present.

WHAT TO DO
(1) *Do not* try to put a dislocated bone back into its place. Unskilled handling can cause extensive damage to nerves and blood vessels. The bone may also be fractured.
(2) Place victim in a comfortable position.
(3) Immobilize the injured part with a splint, pillow, sling, etc., in the position in which it was found. (See Splinting and Other Procedures on pages 83–98.)
(4) Seek medical attention promptly, preferably at the nearest hospital emergency room.
See Also: Broken Bones and Spinal Injuries; Sprains; Wounds

● **Dizziness:** see Shock; Stroke; Unconscious (fainting)
● **Dog bites:** see Bites and Stings (animal)
● **Dope:** see Drug Abuse
● **Downers, abuse:** see Drug Abuse
● **Dressings:** see Part I, page 34

DROWNING

BEWARE

In trying to help someone who is in danger of drowning, remember to be careful of your own safety. In deep water, a drowning person can drag his rescuer under water with him. In an emergency where you must perform the rescue, keep calm and do not overestimate your strength.

HOW TO RESCUE FROM WATER

If a drowning victim is near a pier or the side of a swimming pool, lie down and give the victim your hand or foot and pull him to safety. If the victim is too far away, hold out a life preserver ring, pole, stick, board, rope, chair, tree limb, towel or other object.

If a drowning victim is near a pier, but too far away to reach your hand or foot, lie down and hold out a pole, paddle or life preserver, and pull the victim to safety.

If victim is unconscious or neck or back injury is suspected (from diving, surfboard accident, etc.), place a board (surfboard, table leaf) under victim's head and back while he is still in the water to keep victim from moving, thus preventing further damage to the neck or back. Lift victim out of water on the board. This will help prevent paralysis if neck or back fracture is present.

If victim is out from the shore, wade into the water and extend a pole, board, stick, rope, etc., to victim and pull him to safety. It may be necessary to row a boat to the victim. If so, hand the victim an oar or other suitable object and pull him to the boat. If possible, the victim should hold on to the back of the boat while being rowed to the shore. If this is not possible, pull victim carefully into the boat.

If victim is *not* breathing:
(If victim is breathing, see page 137.)

IMMEDIATE TREATMENT — ABCs

Artificial breathing must be started at once, before victim is completely out of the water, if possible. As soon as the victim's body can be supported, either in a boat or in shallow water, start mouth-to-mouth breathing. (See pages 132–35.) Once out of the water, lay the victim on his back on a firm surface and continue mouth-to-mouth breathing.

Do not waste time trying to drain water from victim's lungs.

I. Open Airway
   (1) Lay victim on his back on a firm rigid surface.
   (2) Quickly clear the mouth and airway of foreign material.
   (3) If there does not appear to be any neck injury, gently tilt victim's head backward by placing one hand beneath the victim's neck and lifting upward. Place the heel of the other hand on the victim's forehead and press downward as the chin is elevated.

(*Continued on page 134.*)

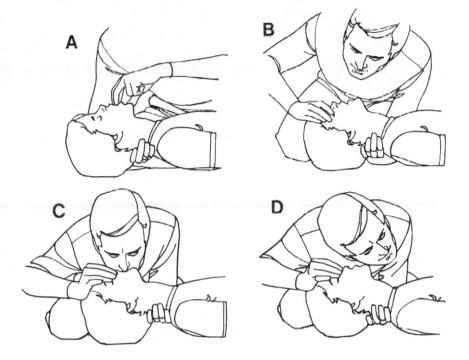

A. Lay victim on his back on a firm, rigid surface. Quickly clear the mouth and airway of foreign material.

B. Tilt the victim's head backward by placing one hand beneath the victim's neck and lifting upward. Place the heel of the other hand on the victim's forehead and press downward as the chin is elevated.

C. With the hand on the victim's forehead, pinch victim's nostrils using your thumb and index finger. Take a deep breath. Place your mouth tightly around the victim's mouth and give four quick breaths. Then give approximately 12 breaths per minute—one breath every five seconds until you see the victim's chest rise.

D. Stop blowing when the victim's chest is expanded. Remove your mouth from the victim's and turn your head toward the victim's chest so that your ear is over the victim's mouth. Listen for air leaving his lungs and watch his chest fall. Repeat breathing procedure.

II. Restore Breathing
   To restore breathing in infants and children,
   see pages 135–36.
   (1) Keep victim's head tilted backward.
   (2) With hand that is on victim's forehead,
       pinch victim's nostrils using your thumb
       and index finger.
   (3) Open your mouth widely and take a deep
       breath.
   (4) Place your mouth tightly around victim's
       mouth and expel four quick breaths.
       (Take a deep breath between each blow.)
       Continue blowing into his mouth at
       approximately 12 breaths per minute.
       Quantity is important so provide plenty
       of air—one breath every five seconds
       until you see the victim's chest rise. (Sec-
       onds are counted "one-one thousand,
       two-one thousand, three-one thousand,"
       etc.)
       Note:
   (5) If the victim's mouth cannot be used due
       to an injury, remove your hand from
       under victim's neck and close his mouth;
       then place your hand over his mouth.
       Open your mouth widely and take a deep
       breath. Place your mouth tightly around
       the victim's nose and blow into it. After
       you exhale, remove your hand from the
       victim's mouth to allow air to escape.
   (6) Moderate resistance will be felt with
       blowing. If chest does not rise, airway is
       not clear and more airway opening is
       needed. Place hands under victim's
       lower jaw and thrust lower jaw forward
       so that it juts out.
   (7) Watch closely to see when victim's chest
       rises, and stop blowing when the chest is
       expanded.
   (8) Remove   your   mouth   from   victim's

mouth or nose and turn your head toward the victim's chest so that your ear is over victim's mouth. Listen for air leaving his lungs and watch his chest fall.

(9) If victim's stomach is bloated with swallowed water, put victim on his stomach. To empty water, place both hands under victim's stomach and lift.

(10) Return victim to his back and continue mouth-to-mouth breathing until victim is breathing well on his own or medical assistance arrives.

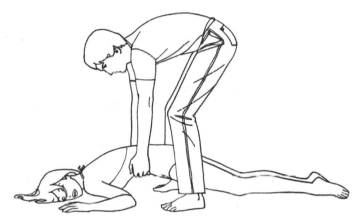

If the victim's stomach is bloated with water, put victim on stomach. To empty water, place both hands under victim's stomach and lift.

III. Restore Breathing in Infants and Children

(1) Mouth-to-mouth or mouth-to-nose artificial breathing is basically the same for infants and small children. However, the head should not be tilted as far back for infants and small children as for adults and large children.

(2) Place your mouth tightly over *both* the mouth and nose of the infant or small child. Breathe small puffs of air into the child's mouth and nose every three sec-

onds (20 breaths per minute) until you see the chest start to rise.

In artificial breathing for children and infants, the head should not be tilted as far back as for adults and large children. Place your mouth tightly over both *the mouth and nose. Breathe small puffs of air into the child's mouth and nose every three seconds until you see the chest rise.*

IV. Restore Circulation
    (1) Check neck artery for pulse. (Check below left nipple in infants.)
    (2) If no pulse is felt, begin cardiac compression. This should be done by those professionally trained and *must* be done in conjunction with artificial breathing. (For one rescuer, give 15 compressions [80 per minute]; then two quick breaths. For two rescuers, give five compressions [60 per minute] for every one breath. Repeat until medical assistance arrives.)

V. Get Medical Assistance
    Call ambulance or paramedics promptly and inform them of drowning. If this is not possible, take victim to the nearest hospital emergency room. Have someone else drive so that

you can continue artificial breathing and cardiac compression if necessary.

CONTINUED CARE

Treat for shock:

(1) Place victim on his side (coma position) with head extended backwards so that fluids will drain.

(2) Keep victim comfortably warm with a blanket, coat or towels. If possible, place blanket beneath a victim lying on a cold wet surface.

(3) Reassure victim. Gentleness, kindness, and understanding play an important role in treating a victim in shock. *Do not* give victim food or water.

If victim is breathing:

IMMEDIATE TREATMENT

(1) Stand by to see that victim continues to breathe on his own.

(2) Place victim on his side (coma position) with head extended backwards so that fluids will drain.

(3) Keep victim comfortably warm.

(4) Reassure victim.

(5) Seek medical attention promptly. *Do not* give victim food or water.

Note:

Cold-water drowning: People who have been submerged in cold water (below 70°F) often can survive *and* without brain damage.* Some victims have been submerged for as long as 38 minutes and have still lived. A reflex most prominent in young children slows the heartbeat and reserves the oxygen in the blood for the heart and brain. Mouth-to-mouth breathing and cardiac compression must be started as soon as possible and continued, often for more than three hours (even if victim appears dead). Victims of cold-water

* As shown in a recent study by Dr. Martin Nemiroff.

drowning do not always respond immediately to mouth-to-mouth resuscitation, but the first-aider should not give up—he should continue resuscitating—even if it is for several hours.

See Also: Part I, pages 20–21; Overexposure: Heat and Cold (cold water drowning); Shock

DRUG ABUSE

ABCs

With all serious injuries, check and maintain an open Airway. Restore Breathing and Circulation if necessary.

Tilt head backward to maintain an open airway.

Drug abuse is the excessive or regular use of a drug outside the usual standards of medical practice. Drug abuse often results in physical and psychological dependence on the drug.

CLUES TO
LOOK FOR

Certain clues may be helpful in identifying a drug abuse emergency and also the drug the victim has taken. Look for needles, eye droppers, teaspoons, pills, capsules, vials, other drug containers and needle marks on the victim's body. Frequent blinking or jerky eye movements are often present in victims of drug overdose. If possible, ask victim what drug he took. Report all information, including first-aid treatment, to the doctor assuming care of the victim.

If victim is seen taking a drug by mouth, is alert, cooperative and in good control of himself, induce vomiting by tickling or touching the back of the victim's throat with your finger. Take care that the victim does not choke on the vomit.

TYPES OF DRUGS

ALCOHOL (alcoholic beverages)

SYMPTOMS

OVERDOSE (Can result from a combination of alcohol and another drug)

(1) Lack of coordination.
(2) Slurred speech.
(3) Abnormal breathing.
(4) Unconsciousness.
(5) Possible coma.
(6) Red streaks in whites of eyeballs.
(7) Odor of alcohol.
(8) Any one or all of the above may be present.

WITHDRAWAL (Body's response when person stops taking drugs to which he has become addicted)

(1) Trembling of hand and head.
(2) Nausea.
(3) Vomiting.
(4) Fear of sounds, simple objects, lights.
(5) Possible hallucinations (seeing and/or hearing objects not present).
(6) High fever.
(7) Unusual behavior.
(8) Any one or all of the above may be present.

IMMEDIATE TREATMENT

OVERDOSE

(1) If victim is sleeping with normal breathing and pulse, no immediate treatment is required. Place victim so that he will not hurt himself.

WITHDRAWAL

(1) Maintain an open airway.
(2) If victim is vomiting, see that he does not choke on vomit.
(3) Seek medical attention promptly.

(2) If victim has abnormal breathing, is unconscious or is in a coma, maintain an open airway and restore breathing if necessary.

(3) Seek medical attention promptly.

(4) Calm and reassure the victim.

CONTINUED CARE

(1) If victim is partially or totally unconscious, place him on his side with head extended backward so that he will not choke on secretions.

(2) Keep victim warm.

(3) See that victim does not harm himself or others.

(4) Calm and reassure victim.

DEPRESSANTS (Sedatives—downers, phenobarbitol, goofballs, yellow jackets, red devils, rainbows, sleeping pills, ludes)

SYMPTOMS

OVERDOSE (Also look for signs of alcohol consumption in combination with sedatives.)

(1) Drunklike behavior.
(2) Slurred speech.
(3) Unconsciousness.
(4) Possible coma.
(5) Staggering walk.
(6) Shallow and slow breathing.
(7) Slow pulse.
(8) Any one or all of the above may be present.

WITHDRAWAL (Symptoms may not all occur at the same time.)

(1) Restlessness, insomnia.
(2) Trembling.
(3) Muscle twitching.
(4) Vomiting.
(5) Convulsions.
(6) Delusions.
(7) Hallucinations.
(8) High temperature.

IMMEDIATE TREATMENT

OVERDOSE

(1) Maintain an open airway and restore breathing if necessary.
(2) Keep victim awake. Use cold wet towel or cloth on victim's face and slap gently.
(3) Keep victim walking if possible— but not to the point of exhaustion.
(4) Seek medical attention promptly.

WITHDRAWAL

(1) Maintain an open airway and restore breathing if necessary.
(2) Seek medical attention promptly.
(3) Calm and reassure the victim.

CONTINUED CARE

OVERDOSE

(1) Keep victim warm.
(2) Calm and reassure victim.

WITHDRAWAL

(1) Keep victim warm.
(2) Calm and reassure victim.

HALLUCINOGENS (LSD, mescaline, psilocybin)

SYMPTOMS

OVERDOSE

(1) Fast heartbeat.
(2) Increased blood pressure.
(3) Enlarged eye pupils.
(4) Reddish face.
(5) Lack of emotional control (periods of laughing and crying; behavior not appropriate for situation or questions you ask).
(6) Delusions (misinterpretation of sounds, movements or objects).
(7) Hallucination, visions (seeing things or hearing sounds that have no factual basis).

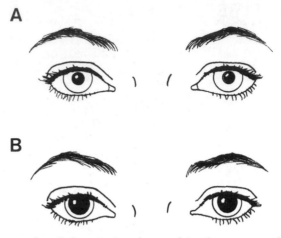

The pupils of the eye are located in the center of the iris.
A. Normal eye pupils (dark circles) are fairly small.
B. Dilated pupils (dark circles) are large and cover a large area of the iris.

---

(8) Depression (appearing sad; slow to move or talk).
(9) Panic, fear, tension.
(10) Varying levels of consciousness.
(11) Disorientation.
(12) Poor recent memory.
(13) Any one or all of the above may be present.

IMMEDIATE TREATMENT

OVERDOSE

(1) See that the victim does not harm himself or others.
(2) Reassure victim and try to talk him down from his experience while in a quiet and peaceful place. Keep your motions slow, voice calm and do not turn away from victim.
(3) Seek medical attention promptly.

INHALANTS (glue, paints and lacquers and their thinners, gasoline, kerosene, nail polish and remover, lighter fluid)

SYMPTOMS OVERDOSE

(1) Drunklike behavior.
(2) Slurred speech.
(3) Happy feeling changing to depression.
(4) Dizziness and unsteadiness.
(5) Double vision.
(6) Chemical odor to breath.
(7) Any one or all of the above may be present.

IMMEDIATE TREATMENT OVERDOSE

(1) Remove bag or other object used for sniffing from victim's reach.
(2) Maintain an open airway and restore breathing if necessary.
(3) Seek medical attention promptly.

MARIJUANA (cannabis, grass)

SYMPTOMS OVERDOSE

(1) Reddening of the eyes.
(2) Dizziness.
(3) Lack of coordination.
(4) Sleepiness.
(5) Fast heartbeat.
(6) Increased appetite.
(7) Happiness, cheerfulness, silliness, or fearfulness.
(8) Talkativeness (speech may be slow).
(9) Confusion over time and space.
(10) Poor recent memory.
(11) Any one or all of the above may be present.

WHAT TO DO OVERDOSE

(1) Normally there is no need for treatment except to see that the victim does not harm himself.
(2) If victim experiences an unpleasant reaction, calm and reassure the victim and try to talk

him down from his experience while in a quiet and peaceful place.

(3) It is advisable to seek medical attention in case other drugs were also taken.

NARCOTICS (opium, morphine, heroin, codeine, etc.)

SYMPTOMS

OVERDOSE	WITHDRAWAL
(1) Extreme lack of energy.	(1) Nervousness, restlessness.
(2) Sleep, possibly leading to coma.	(2) Abdominal cramping.
(3) Heavy sweating.	(3) Hot and cold flashes.
(4) Low body temperature.	(4) Sweating.
(5) Breathing slows and may possibly stop.	(5) Tears.
	(6) Runny nose.
	(7) Yawning.
(6) Muscles very relaxed.	(8) Muscle aches.
(7) Pupils of eyes become very small.	(9) Vomiting.
	(10) Loss of appetite.
	(11) Weight loss.
(8) Very slow pulse.	(12) Enlarged eye pupils.
(9) Any one or all of the above may be present.	(13) Rapid breathing.
	(14) Increased blood pressure.
	(15) Rise in body temperature.
	(16) Craving for drug.
	(17) Any one or all of the above may be present.

IMMEDIATE TREATMENT

OVERDOSE	WITHDRAWAL
(1) Maintain an open airway and restore breathing if necessary.	(1) Victim may need medical attention if discomfort is severe.

(2) Keep victim
awake. Use cold
wet towel or cloth
on victim's face
and slap gently.
(3) Keep victim walk-
ing if possible.
(4) Seek medical at-
tention promptly.
(5) Calm and reassure
the victim.

STIMULANTS (uppers, pep pills, Benzedrine, bennies, whites, Dexedrine, dexies, speed, crystal)

SYMPTOMS

OVERDOSE	WITHDRAWAL
(1) Mental confusion.	(1) Extreme lack of energy.
(2) Disorganization.	(2) Depression.
(3) Repeating particular act over and over.	(3) Extreme hunger.
(4) Irritableness.	(4) Hallucinations.
(5) Fear.	(5) Any one or all of the above may be present.
(6) Suspiciousness.	
(7) Aggressive behavior.	
(8) Overly active.	
(9) Any one or all of the above may be present.	

WHAT TO DO

OVERDOSE	WITHDRAWAL
(1) Keep victim from harming himself or others.	(1) Advise psychiatric attention.
(2) Advise psychiatric attention.	

TRANQUILIZERS (Librium, Valium, Mellaril, Quaalude)   (Continued on next page.)

SYMPTOMS

OVERDOSE

(1) Unconsciousness.
(2) Possible coma.
(3) Decrease in body temperature and blood pressure.
(4) Any one or all of the above may be present.

WITHDRAWAL (Not all symptoms occur at the same time.)

(1) Restlessness, insomnia.
(2) Trembling.
(3) Muscle twitching.
(4) Vomiting.
(5) Convulsions.
(6) Delusions.
(7) Hallucinations.
(8) Any one or all of the above may be present.

IMMEDIATE TREATMENT

OVERDOSE

(1) Maintain an open airway and restore breathing if necessary.
(2) Keep victim awake. Use cold wet towel or cloth on victim's face and slap gently.
(3) Keep victim walking if possible.
(4) Seek medical attention promptly.

WITHDRAWAL

(1) Maintain an open airway and restore breathing if necessary.
(2) Seek medical attention promptly.

CONTINUED CARE

OVERDOSE

(1) Keep victim warm.
(2) Reassure victim.

WITHDRAWAL

(1) Keep victim warm.
(2) Reassure victim.

See Also: Convulsions; Poisons; Suicide, Threatened; Unconscious

- **Drug rash:** see Rashes (drug rash)
- **Drunkenness:** see Drug Abuse
- **Dysentery:** see Diarrhea

EAR INJURIES AND EARACHES

BLEEDING FROM INSIDE THE EAR

A ruptured eardrum can be caused by a loud blast, an infection, diving into water, falls from water skiing, objects poked into the ear or from a head injury. Bleeding or other fluids from the ear canal may mean a serious head injury.

SYMPTOMS
(1) Bleeding from inside the ear canal.
(2) Pain.
(3) Hearing loss.
(4) Any one or all of the above may be present.

IMMEDIATE TREATMENT
(1) If bleeding is due to a head injury with a possible skull fracture, treat head injury first. (See Head Injuries on pages 166–69.)
(2) *Do not* put anything into the ear.
(3) *Do not* try to stop the flow of blood from the ear canal.
(4) Loosely cover the outside of the ear with a bandage or cloth to catch the flow of blood.
(5) Place the victim on his injured side so that the affected ear is downward, allowing blood to drain. The victim should not be moved if a serious neck, head or back injury is suspected unless his life is in jeopardy.
(6) Seek medical attention promptly.

FOREIGN OBJECTS INSIDE THE EAR

Children often put objects into their ears. The most common objects are peas, beans, beads, paper and cotton. Insects may also get trapped inside the ear.

WHAT TO DO
(1) If an insect inside the ear is alive and buzzing, put several drops of warm oil (baby, mineral or olive oil) into the ear to kill the insect. This is the only time putting oil into the ear is justified. Seek medical attention for removal of the insect.

(2) Other small objects trapped inside the ear need medical attention for removal. The only possible exception is paper or cotton *if* it is *clearly* visible outside the ear canal. One attempt to remove it may be carefully made with tweezers. A doctor should be seen, however, to make sure all of it is removed.

(3) *Do not* put water or oil into the ears to attempt to flush out the object. This may cause object to swell and make removal more difficult.

FROSTBITE

SYMPTOMS
(1) In the earliest stages the skin appears red. Pain is often present.

(2) As frostbite develops, the skin becomes white or grayish yellow and appears waxy.

(3) Ears feel very cold and numb.

(4) Pain disappears.

(5) Possible blisters.

(6) Often the victim is not aware that he has frostbite until someone else notices his symptoms.

(7) Any one or all of the above may be present.

IMMEDIATE TREATMENT

(1) While outside, cover the ears with extra clothing or a warm cloth.
(2) *Do not* rub the ears with snow or anything else.
(3) Bring the victim inside promptly.
(4) Frostbitten ears must be rewarmed rapidly.
(5) Gently wrap ears in warm materials.
(6) *Do not* use heat lamps, hot water bottles or heating pads.
(7) *Do not* allow victim to place frostbitten ears near a hot stove or radiator.
(8) *Do not* break blisters.
(9) Stop rewarming process when the skin becomes pink.
(10) Seek medical attention promptly.

CONTINUED CARE

(1) Give victim warm drinks such as tea, coffee or soup.
(2) *Do not* give the victim alcoholic beverages.
(3) Take extreme care that frostbitten ears are not refrozen after they have thawed.

EARACHES

There are many causes for pain in the ear. One of the most common is an infection of the outer ear caused by swimming in contaminated water. This earache is also called "swimmer's ear." Symptoms of "swimmer's ear" may include pain (particularly when the ear is pulled), itching and a discharge from the ear. This condition requires medical attention.

Earaches in the middle ear often follow respiratory infections. Germs in the nose and throat move through the Eustachian tube to the middle ear. Children are particularly subject to middle ear infections because their Eustachian tubes are shorter than those of adults. Infected tonsils may also cause a middle ear infection. Symptoms of middle ear infection may include pain, fever and a discharge from the ear. An infant with an ear infection cries loudly, particularly when lying down, pulls or bats at his ear or turns his head from side to side.

Medical attention is required for treatment of middle ear infections.

Note:

Do not put Q-tips®, hairpins, matches or anything else in the ear.

See Also: Head Injuries

● **Eating difficulty:** see Choking

● **Eclampsia:** see Headaches (headaches in pregnancy)

● **Ectopic pregnancy:** see Abdominal Pain (tubal pregnancy)

● **Elbow injury:** see Broken Bones and Spinal Injuries; Dislocations; Sprains

ELECTRIC SHOCK

BEWARE

Person who is trying to help:

It is extremely important to remain calm. There is a risk of injury to the person who is trying to help. *Do not* touch the victim directly until the electric current is turned off or the victim is no longer in contact with it. Otherwise, the first-aider risks electrocution to himself. Victims who have been struck by lightning, however, may be touched immediately.

REMOVAL OF VICTIM FROM SOURCE OF ELECTRICITY

(1) If possible, turn off the electric current by removing the fuse or by pulling the main switch. If this is not possible, or victim is outside, have someone call the electric company to cut off the electricity.

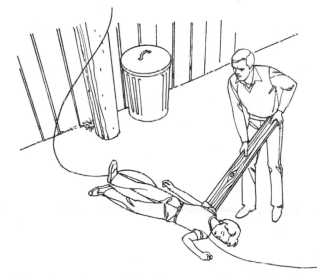

Be extremely careful when removing victim from a live wire. Stand on dry *area. Push victim away from the wire with a* dry *board or other* dry *object. Never use anything metallic or wet.* Do not *touch victim until he is free from the wire.*

(2) If it is necessary to remove the victim from a live wire, be extremely careful. Stand on something *dry* such as a newspaper, board, blanket, rubber mat or cloth, and, if possible, wear *dry* gloves.

(3) Push the victim away from the wire with a *dry* board, stick or broom handle, or pull victim away with a *dry* rope looped around victim's arm or leg. *Never* use anything metallic, wet or damp. Do not touch victim until he is free from the wire.

If victim is not breathing:

IMMEDIATE TREATMENT — ABCs

I. Open Airway

(1) Lay victim on his back on a firm stiff surface such as the floor or the ground.

(2) Quickly clear the mouth and airway of foreign material.

(Continued on page 153.)

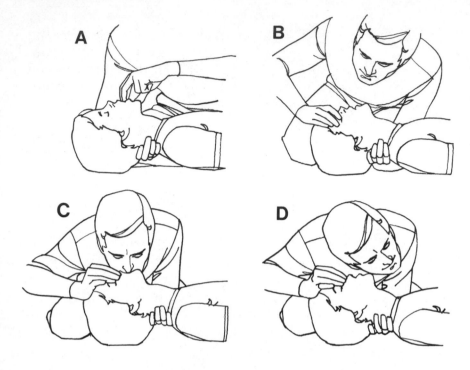

A. Lay victim on his back on a firm, rigid surface. Quickly clear the mouth and airway of foreign material.

B. Tilt the victim's head backward by placing one hand beneath the victim's neck and lifting upward. Place the heel of the other hand on the victim's forehead and press downward as the chin is elevated.

C. With the hand on the victim's forehead, pinch victim's nostrils using your thumb and index finger. Take a deep breath. Place your mouth tightly around the victim's mouth and give four quick breaths. Then give approximately 12 breaths per minute—one breath every five seconds until you see the victim's chest rise.

D. Stop blowing when the victim's chest is expanded. Remove your mouth from the victim's and turn your head toward the victim's chest so that your ear is over the victim's mouth. Listen for air leaving his lungs and watch his chest fall. Repeat breathing procedure.

(3) If there is no neck injury, gently tilt victim's head backward by placing one hand beneath the victim's neck and lifting upward. Place the heel of the other hand on the victim's forehead and press downward as the chin is elevated.

II. Restore Breathing

To restore breathing in infants and children, see pages 154–55.

(1) Keep victim's head tilted backward.

(2) With hand that is placed on victim's forehead, pinch nostrils using the thumb and index finger.

(3) Open your mouth widely and take a deep breath.

(4) Place your mouth tightly around victim's mouth and give four quick breaths. Then blow into his mouth approximately 12 breaths per minute for an adult. Quantity is important so provide plenty of air—one breath every five seconds until you see the victim's chest rise. (Seconds are counted "one-one thousand, two-one thousand, three-one thousand," etc.)
Note:

(5) If the victim's mouth cannot be used due to injury, remove hand under victim's neck and close his mouth; then place your hand over his mouth. Open your mouth widely and take a deep breath. Place your mouth tightly around the victim's nose and blow into it. After you exhale, remove your hand from the victim's mouth to allow air to escape.

(6) Moderate resistance will be felt with blowing. If chest does not rise, airway is not clear and more airway opening is needed. Place hands under victim's lower jaw and thrust lower jaw forward so that it juts out.

(7) Watch closely to see when victim's chest rises, and stop blowing when the chest is expanded.

(8) Remove your mouth from victim's mouth or nose and turn your head so that your ear is over victim's mouth. Listen for air leaving his lungs.

(9) Repeat blowing air into victim until he is breathing well on his own or medical assistance arrives. In electric shock artificial respiration may be required for a long time. Don't get discouraged.

III. Restore Breathing in Infants and Children

(1) Mouth-to-mouth or mouth-to-nose artificial respiration is basically the same for infants and small children. However, the head should not be tilted as far back for infants and small children as for adults and large children.

(2) Place your mouth tightly over *both* the mouth and nose of the infant or small

In artificial breathing for children and infants, the head should not be tilted as far back as for adults and large children. Place your mouth tightly over both *the mouth and nose. Breathe small puffs of air into the child's mouth and nose every three seconds until you see the chest rise.*

child. Breathe small puffs of air into the child's mouth and nose every three seconds (20 breaths per minute) until you see the chest begin to rise on each breath you blow in.

IV. Restore Circulation

(1) Check neck artery for pulse. Check below left nipple in infants.

(2) If no pulse is felt, begin cardiac compression. This should be done by those professionally trained and *must* be done in conjunction with artificial respiration. (For one rescuer, give 15 compressions [80 per minute]; then two quick breaths. For two rescuers, give five compressions [60 per minute] for every one breath. Repeat until medical attention arrives.)

V. Get Medical Assistance

Call ambulance or paramedics promptly and inform medics of electric shock. If this is not possible, take victim to the nearest hospital emergency room. Have someone else drive so that you can continue artificial breathing and cardiac compression if necessary.

See Also: Part I, pages 21–22; Burns; Shock; Unconscious

● **Electrocution:** see Electric Shock

● **Emergency medical identification:** see Part I, page 6

● **Emergency rooms:** see Part I, pages 43–45

● **Epileptic seizures:** see Part I, page 33; Convulsions (epileptic seizure)

EYE INJURIES

CHEMICAL BURNS

Drain cleaner, bleach or other cleaning solutions are some chemical agents that can burn the eye.

Chemical burns of the eye are very serious and may lead to blindness if immediate action is not taken. Speed in removing a chemical agent is vital. Damage can occur in one to five minutes.

IMMEDIATE TREATMENT

(1) Before calling a doctor, immediately flush eye with large quantities of cool running water for about ten minutes to rinse out offending agent. Use milk if water is not available. Hold victim's head under a faucet, with eyelids held open, and allow the water to run from the inside corner (next to the nose) outward so that the water flows over the entire eye and so that the chemical does not get in the unaffected eye. If both eyes are affected, let water flow over both or quickly alternate from one eye to the other. Be sure to lift and separate eyelids so that all parts of the eye will be reached by the water.

(2) Another method is to place the top of the victim's face in a bowl or sink filled with water with eyes in water, and have victim move eyelids up and down.

(3) If victim is lying down, pour large quantities of water from a container from the inside corner of the eye outward, keeping the eyelids open. Keep repeating this procedure.

(4) Cover the injured eye or eyes with a pad of sterile gauze or a clean folded handkerchief, and bandage in place. Eyelids should be closed.

(5) *Do not* allow victim to rub his eyes.

(6) Seek medical attention immediately, preferably from a physician who is an eye specialist

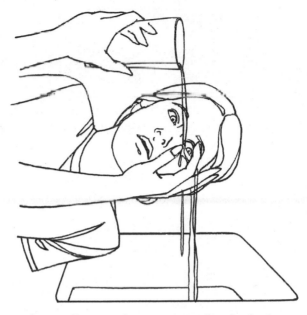

Before calling a doctor, immediately flush eye with large quantities of cool running water for about ten minutes. Allow water to run from the inside corner outward. Lift and separate eyelids so that all parts of the eye will be covered by the water.

(preferably an ophthalmologist) or at the nearest hospital emergency room.

FOREIGN BODIES IN THE EYE

BEWARE

Never attempt to remove any particle that is sticking into the eyeball. Seek immediate medical attention for such injuries. See Immediate Treatment that follows.

Particles such as eyelashes, cinders or specks that are resting or floating on the eyeball or inside of the eyelid may be carefully removed.

SYMPTOMS

(1) Pain.
(2) Burning sensation.

(3) Tearing.
(4) Redness of the eye.
(5) Sensitivity to light.

If foreign body is *sticking into* the eyeball:

IMMEDIATE TREATMENT

(1) *Do not* allow victim to rub his eyes.
(2) Wash your hands with soap and water before carefully examining victim's eyes.
(3) If foreign body is sticking into the eyeball, *do not* attempt to remove it.
(4) Gently cover *both* eyes (because when one moves so does the other) with sterile or clean compresses and bandage lightly in place around victim's head. If compresses are not available, use a scarf, large cloth napkin or other suitable material and tie around victim's head.
(5) Seek medical attention promptly, preferably from a physician who is an eye specialist (preferably an ophthalmologist) or at the nearest hospital emergency room. Keep victim lying down on his back while riding to the hospital. Use a stretcher if possible.

If foreign body is *resting* or *floating on* the eyeball or inside of the eyelid:

WHAT TO DO

(1) *Do not* allow victim to rub his eyes.
(2) Wash your hands with soap and water before carefully examining victim's eyes.
(3) Gently pull upper eyelid down over lower eyelid and hold for a moment. This causes tears to flow which will hopefully wash out the particle.
(4) If particle has not been removed, fill medicine dropper with warm water and squeeze water over the eye to flush out particle. If medicine dropper is not available, hold head under gentle stream of running water to flush out particle in eye.

(5) If still unsuccessful, gently pull lower eyelid down. If foreign body can be seen on the inside of the lower lid, carefully lift particle out with a moistened corner of a clean handkerchief, cloth or facial tissue.

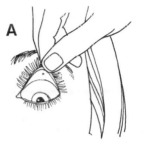
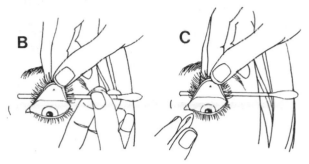

A. *Note particle resting on inside of upper lid. Victim must look downward during procedure to remove particle. Hold lashes of the upper eyelid and pull downward.*
B. *While holding the eyelid down, place a kitchen match or Q-tip® horizontally across the outside of the lid and flip the eyelid backward over the stick.*
C. *Carefully remove particle with moistened corner of handkerchief, etc.*

(6) If speck is not visible on the lower lid, check the inside of upper lid. This can be done by first holding the lashes of the upper eyelid and pulling downward. Victim must look downward during entire procedure. While holding the eyelid down, place a kitchen match or Q-tip® horizontally across the outside of the lid and flip the eyelid backward over the stick. (Victim can help by holding the stick.) Carefully remove the particle with moistened corner of handkerchief, cloth or facial tissue.

(7) If particle still remains, gently cover the eye with a sterile or clean compress.

(8) Seek medical attention promptly.

CUTS

Any cuts to the eye, including the eyelid, can be very serious and could lead to blindness if immediate action is not taken.

IMMEDIATE TREATMENT

(1) Cover the injured eye with a sterile pad or gauze or a clean folded cloth and bandage in place, but apply no pressure. Also cover the other uninjured eye to prevent eyeball movement.

(2) Seek medical attention immediately, preferably from a physician who is an eye specialist (preferably an ophthalmologist) or at the nearest hospital emergency room. Transport victim lying down flat on his back if possible.

BLUNT INJURIES (Black Eye)

Any injury resulting from a hard direct blow to the eye such as a moving ball, a fist, etc., needs medical attention by an opthalmologist even though the injury may not look serious. There may be internal bleeding in the eye.

IMMEDIATE TREATMENT

(1) Apply *cold* compresses to the injured eye.
(2) If possible, keep victim lying down with eyes closed.
(3) Seek medical attention.

CONTACT LENSES

In eye injuries in which the victim is wearing contact lenses, the lenses should be removed by a physician, preferably an ophthalmologist, as soon as possible.

COMMON EYE INFECTIONS

Pink Eye (Conjunctivitis)

Pink eye is an infection of the eye that is usually caused by fungus, bacteria, allergies or chemicals. It may affect one or both eyes. Certain forms of pink eye are very contagious.

SYMPTOMS

(1) Redness of the white portion of the eye.
(2) Watery or sticky discharge (colored—yellow, green or brown) from the eye.
(3) Upper and lower eyelashes may stick together, particularly upon rising in the morning.
(4) Sensation of something in the eye.

WHAT TO DO

(1) Consult a physician.
(2) Place ice cube in a plastic bag and hold over eyelid. This offers *temporary* relief of pain.

Stye

A stye is an inflammation of the glands of the eyelid.

SYMPTOMS

(1) Tender, red bumps near the edge of the eyelid.

WHAT TO DO

(1) Apply warm water compresses to the affected area several times a day.
(2) *Do not* try to "pop" this pimplelike bump.
(3) If stye persists longer than several days or recurs, seek medical attention.
Note:
Any sudden pain in the eyes without recent injury or a sudden blurring or loss of vision requires immediate medical attention.
See Also: Head Injuries

● **Fainting:** see Part I, page 33; Overexposure: Heat and Cold; Poisons; Shock; Stroke; Unconscious (fainting)

● **Falls:** see Broken Bones and Spinal Injuries; Dislocations; Minor Injuries; Sprains; Strains

FEVER

A fever is the body's way of indicating that something is wrong within it. Most commonly, a fever indicates that an infection is present. It is the body's defensive mechanism to combat infection.

ADULTS

The average normal temperature taken by mouth is 98.6°F (37°C). A rectal temperature is one degree higher than a normal oral temperature. Individual normal temperatures may run slightly above or below the average. Individual temperatures may also vary throughout the day, running lower in the morning and higher in the evening. Slight changes in temperature (other than normal variations during the day) are usually not significant. A major increase in temperature (to approximately 104°F or over) may indicate a serious condition. However, temperatures well below normal may also be significant. (See also Overexposure: Heat and Cold.)

A doctor should always be called if a fever suddenly changes from slight (99°F to 100°F) to high (104°F) and persists. If the victim is an infant and the doctor cannot be reached, take the infant to the nearest hospital emergency room. The same steps should be taken if a fever is present for no obvious reason and it persists. (It is best not to take any medication to reduce the fever in this case, as this may give a false sense of well-being and discourage you from consulting a doctor.)

WHAT TO DO Aspirin and other similar medications are helpful in reducing a fever. Also, remove excessive clothing and/or remove the victim from an unusually warm environment. Follow the package recommendations or a doctor's instructions in determining the dosage of aspirin, etc., to be taken.

INFANTS AND CHILDREN

A normal temperature taken rectally in infants and small children is usually below 100°F. (Rectal temperatures run about one degree higher than oral temperatures.) Children can run high fevers without being seriously ill. It is always best, however, to report any fever over 101°F to the doctor, particularly if the child does not feel, look or act well. Report any other symptoms the child might have to the doctor.

WHAT TO DO (1) It is always best to check with the doctor before giving medication to an infant or small child, particularly one under 1 year of age.
(2) Give the child plenty of fluids to drink.
(3) Have the child rest, in bed if possible.
(4) High fevers (104°F or over) can be reduced by sponging the child with tepid (warm) water and letting the water evaporate on the skin. Recheck temperature every 25 to 30 minutes. Continue sponge bath until rectal temperature is below 102°F. Be careful, however, that the child does not become chilled.

HOW TO READ A THERMOMETER

Most temperatures are taken by mouth with an oral thermometer. People with mouth injuries, infants and small children should have their temperature taken by rectum with a rectal thermometer. In oral thermometers, the bulb containing

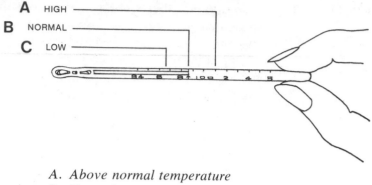

A. *Above normal temperature*
B. *Normal average temperature*
C. *Below normal temperature*

mercury is long and thin; the bulb in a rectal thermometer is short and fat.

To read either type of thermometer, hold the
end without the bulb between the thumb and the
first finger. Use good light. Look through the
pointed edge toward the flat side until you see a
thin silver or red line coming out of the bulb. Ro-
tate the thermometer slightly if the silver line is
not visible. The temperature reading is at the end
of the silver line. The long lines mark the degrees
of temperature and the short lines indicate two-
tenths of a degree. An arrow points to the normal reading of 98.6°F (37°C). Readings higher
than this indicate a fever, except in rectal temperature, which is one degree higher.

Before taking a temperature, the thermometer
must be shaken down so that the silver or red line
reads below the 98.6°F (37°C) mark to approximately 95°F. Hold the thermometer as described
above. Shake the thermometer sharply downward
with a snapping wrist movement. Read the thermometer to make sure the mercury is shaken
down.

Personal property of George Wyman

HOW TO TAKE A TEMPERATURE

If using an oral thermometer, insert the bulb under the victim's tongue. Keep the thermometer in place for at least three minutes. Warn the victim not to talk or bite on the thermometer. *Do not* take a temperature for at least 30 minutes after the victim has taken a bath, smoked, eaten hot or cold foods or drunk water; this can affect the temperature reading.

If you have difficulty reading the thermometer, put it away until someone else can read it. The temperature reading will remain marked until the thermometer is shaken down.

To take a rectal temperature, place the infant or young child on his stomach on a firm surface. Separate the buttocks so that the rectum is visible. Lubricate the bulb end of the thermometer with cold cream or petroleum jelly and gently insert into the rectum about 1 inch. Never use force. If you meet resistance, simply change direction of the thermometer slightly. Put a hand on the child's buttocks and hold the thermometer firmly between your fingers. Leave the thermometer in for three minutes. If the child struggles, quiet him and place the other hand on the small of his back.

See Also: Part I, pages 8–9; Chills

● **Finger injury:** see Part I (Loss of Limb), page 32; Broken Bones and Spinal Injuries; Dislocations; Minor Injuries (injured fingertip)

● **Fire:** see Burns

● **Fireworks explosion:** see Wounds (puncture wounds)

● **First-aid kit:** see Part I, page 7

● **Fishhook injury:** see Minor Injuries (fishhook injury)

● **Fit:** see Convulsions

Flu: see Abdominal Pain; Chills; Diarrhea

Food poisoning: see Poisons (food poisoning)

Foot injury: see Broken Bones and Spinal Injuries; Muscle Aches and Pains

Fractures: see Broken Bones and Spinal Injuries; Dislocations; Head Injuries

Freezing: see Part I, page 31; Overexposure: Heat and Cold (cold injuries)

Frostbite: see Ear Injuries and Earaches (frostbite); Overexposure: Heat and Cold

Gagging: see Choking; Vomiting

Gas inhalation: see Poisons (poisoning from smoke, chemical or gas fumes); Unconscious

Gas leaks: see Part I, page 23

Gasoline, inhalant: see Drug Abuse

German measles: see Rashes (diseases)

Glue, inhalant: see Drug Abuse

Grass: see Drug Abuse

Hallucinations: see Drug Abuse

Hand injury: see Broken Bones and Spinal Injuries

HEAD INJURIES

ABCs
With all serious injuries maintain an open Airway. Restore Breathing and Circulation if necessary.

Tilt head backward to maintain an open airway.

BEWARE

All head injuries must be taken seriously as they can result in brain or spinal cord damage. Any victim who is found unconscious must be assumed to have a head injury until proven otherwise by medical personnel. Most head injuries are caused by a fall, a blow to the head, a collision, or sudden stopping as in an automobile accident.

SYMPTOMS

Some symptoms may not occur immediately, but those to look for are:

(1) A cut, bruise, lump or depression in the scalp.
(2) Possible unconsciousness, confusion or drowsiness.
(3) Bleeding from the nose, ear or mouth.
(4) Clear or bloody fluid flowing from the nose or ears.
(5) A pale *or* reddish face.
(6) Headache.
(7) Vomiting.
(8) Convulsions.
(9) Pupils of the eyes unequal in size.
(10) Difficulty in speech.
(11) Restlessness and (possibly) confused behavior.
(12) A change in pulse rate.
(13) Any one or all of the above may be present.

IMMEDIATE TREATMENT

(1) Maintain an open airway. Be very careful as there may be a possibility of a broken neck. Restore breathing if necessary by mouth-to-mouth resuscitation.
(2) *Do not* move the victim more than is absolutely necessary. Handle the victim very carefully.
(3) Keep victim lying down if possible.
(4) If victim's face is red and there is *no* evidence of a neck or back injury (with a neck or back injury the victim cannot move his arms,

hands, fingers and/or legs, feet and toes; there will be pain in neck or back), elevate head *and* shoulders slightly with a pillow or rolled blanket but be sure breathing is not impaired.

(5) If victim's face is pale, keep the head level with the rest of his body.

(6) If there is no evidence of a neck or back injury, turn the victim's head to the side to allow secretions to drain.

(7) Control serious bleeding. (See Bleeding on pages 72–80.) Gently apply compress to bleeding area and bandage in place.

(8) *Do not* give victim anything by mouth.

(9) Seek medical attention promptly, preferably at the nearest hospital emergency room. If someone else other than trained medical personnel must take victim to the hospital, transport victim lying down. Place pads or other suitable material on each side of victim's head to keep it from moving side to side.

CONTINUED CARE

(1) Keep victim comfortably warm.

(2) Keep notes on length and extent of unusual behavior or unconsciousness.

Note:

All victims of head injuries should seek prompt medical attention particularly if victim was or is unconscious. However, if victim did not lose consciousness at the time of the injury and did not seek medical attention, delayed symptoms of brain damage should be watched closely for several days. If any of the symptoms of brain damage appear, particularly unconsciousness, change in pulse, difficulty in breathing, convulsions, severe vomiting, unequal eye pupils or a generally poor or ill appearance, medical attention must be sought promptly.

CUTS OF THE SCALP

Cuts of the scalp may bleed heavily even if the wound is minor.

If the cut is *severe* or there is the possibility of *skull fracture:*

IMMEDIATE
TREATMENT

(1) *Do not* clean the wound or remove any foreign bodies from the scalp.
(2) Gently apply a sterile compress and bandage in place. If bleeding persists, apply pressure firmly about the wound.
(3) Seek medical attention promptly.

If the cut is *minor:*

WHAT TO DO

(1) Control bleeding with pressure.
(2) Clean the wound with soap and water.
(3) Apply a Band-Aid®.

Note:
   With any cut, puncture, etc., victim should consult physician about necessity for a tetanus shot.
See Also: Part I, pages 24–27; Broken Bones and Spinal Injuries; Convulsions; Dental Emergencies; Ear Injuries and Earaches; Eye Injuries; Unconscious; Wounds

● **Hearing loss:** see Ear Injuries and Earaches

HEADACHES

Headaches are a very common complaint. Most headaches are caused by emotional tension and can usually be relieved by aspirin or other similar medication, and rest. Applying heat to the back of the neck is often helpful. Massaging the neck muscles and the scalp also helps relieve headache pain.

Other causes of headache include viral infections, sinus infections, allergies, high blood pressure, stroke, brain tumor, meningitis and head injuries. Any severe or persistent headache requires medical attention.

HEADACHES IN PREGNANCY

Severe or persistent headaches in pregnancy can be serious to both the mother and the baby. They may indicate a condition known as toxemia. Other symptoms such as swelling in the face and fingers, blurred vision and rapid weight gain are also usually present. Toxemia occurs during the latter part of the pregnancy. Any severe or persistent headache during pregnancy requires prompt medical attention.

See Also: Part I, page 10; Drug Abuse; Head Injury; Overexposure: Heat and Cold; Poisons; Stroke

HEART ATTACK

A heart attack is a life-threatening emergency. It occurs when there is not enough blood and oxygen reaching a portion of the heart due to a narrowing or obstruction of the coronary arteries that supply the heart muscle. If this lack of blood and oxygen is prolonged, a part of the heart muscle will die.

SYMPTOMS

(1) Central chest pain that is severe, crushing (not sharp), constant and lasts for several minutes.

(2) Chest pain that moves through the chest to either arm, shoulder, neck, jaw, mid-back or pit of stomach.

(3) Heavy sweating.
(4) Nausea and vomiting.
(5) Extreme weakness.
(6) Victim is anxious and afraid.
(7) Skin is pale. Fingernails and lips may be blue.
(8) Extreme shortness of breath (mild to severe).
(9) Pain may be mistaken for indigestion.
(10) Any one or all of the above may be present.

If victim is *unconscious* and *not breathing,* or is having difficulty in breathing: (If victim is conscious, see pages 174–75.)

IMMEDIATE TREATMENT— ABCs

I. Open Airway
(1) Lay victim on his back on a firm rigid surface such as the floor or the ground.
(2) Quickly clear the mouth and airway of foreign material.
(3) Gently tilt the victim's head backward by placing one hand beneath the victim's neck and lifting upward, and by placing the heel of the other hand on the victim's forehead and pressing downward as the chin is elevated.

II. Restore Breathing
(1) Keep victim's head tilted backward.
(2) With hand that is placed on victim's forehead, pinch victim's nostrils using the thumb and index finger.
(3) Open your mouth widely and take a deep breath.
(4) Place your mouth tightly around victim's mouth and give four quick breaths. Then blow into his mouth approximately 12 breaths per minute. Quantity is important so provide plenty of air—one breath every five seconds until you see the victim's chest rise. (Seconds are counted

(*Continued on page 173.*)

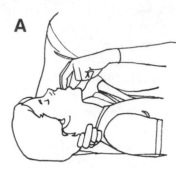

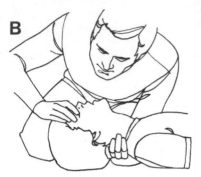

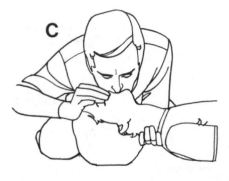

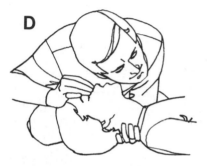

A. *Lay victim on his back on a firm, rigid surface. Quickly clear the mouth and airway of foreign material.*

B. *Tilt the victim's head backward by placing one hand beneath the victim's neck and lifting upward. Place the heel of the other hand on the victim's forehead and press downward as the chin is elevated.*

C. *With the hand on the victim's forehead, pinch victim's nostrils using your thumb and index finger. Take a deep breath. Place your mouth tightly around the victim's mouth and give four quick breaths. Then give approximately 12 breaths per minute —one breath every five seconds until you see the victim's chest rise.*

D. *Stop blowing when the victim's chest is expanded. Remove your mouth from the victim's and turn your head toward the victim's chest so that your ear is over the victim's mouth. Listen for air leaving his lungs and watch his chest fall. Repeat breathing procedure.*

"one-one thousand, two-one thousand, three-one thousand," etc.)

Note:

(5) If the victim's mouth cannot be used, remove hand under victim's neck and close his mouth. Open your mouth widely and take a deep breath. Place your mouth tightly around the victim's nose and blow into it. After you exhale, remove your hand from the victim's mouth for air to escape.

(6) Moderate resistance will be felt with blowing. If chest does not rise, airway is unclear and more airway opening is needed. Place hands under the victim's lower jaw and thrust lower jaw forward so that it juts out.

(7) Watch closely to see when victim's chest rises, and stop blowing when the chest is expanded.

(8) Remove your mouth from victim's mouth or nose and turn your head so that your ear is over victim's mouth. Listen for air leaving his lungs.

(9) Repeat blowing instructions until victim is breathing well on his own or until medical assistance arrives.

III. Restore Circulation

(1) Check wrist or neck artery for pulse.

(2) If no pulse is present, begin cardiac compressions. This should be done by those professionally trained and *must* be done in conjunction with artificial breathing. (For one rescuer, give 15 compressions [80 per minute]; then two quick breaths. For two rescuers, give five compressions [60 per minute] for every one breath. Repeat until medical assistance arrives.)

IV. Summon Medical Assistance

Call ambulance or paramedics and inform

medics of possible heart attack and of need for oxygen. If this is not possible, take victim to the nearest hospital emergency room. Have someone else drive so that you can continue artificial breathing and circulation if necessary.

CONTINUED CARE

(1) Loosen any tight clothing, particularly around victim's neck.
(2) Keep victim comfortably warm by covering his body with a blanket or coat.
(3) Reassure victim.
(4) *Do not* give victim anything to eat or drink and do not apply smelling salts.

If victim is *conscious* at onset of heart attack:

IMMEDIATE TREATMENT

(1) Gently place victim in a comfortable position. This will either be sitting up or a semisitting position. A pillow or two may allow greater comfort. Victim should not lie down flat as this position makes breathing more difficult.
(2) Loosen tight clothing, particularly around victim's neck.
(3) Keep victim comfortably warm by covering his body with a blanket or coat.
(4) Calm and reassure the victim.
(5) Call ambulance or paramedics and inform medics of possible heart attack and of need for oxygen. If this is not possible, take victim to the nearest hospital emergency room or physician promptly.

If you are *alone* and think you're having a heart attack:

WHAT TO DO

(1) Call an ambulance or paramedics immediately and inform medics of possible heart attack and of need for oxygen.
(2) Get into a comfortable position. This will ei-

ther be sitting up or a semisitting position. A pillow or two may allow greater comfort.

(3) Loosen tight clothing, particularly around your neck.

(4) Keep yourself comfortably warm.

(5) Do not eat or drink anything.

Note:

Not all chest pains are symptoms of a heart attack. Chest pains can be due to strenuous exercise, inflamed nerves, infections, muscle spasms or excitement. These pains are usually sharp and may repeat but usually last only a few seconds. Chest pains may also be caused by tension, pneumonia, fractured ribs, gas, bruises, strained muscles or shingles. But it is always a good idea to report any chest pains to a doctor.

See Also: Part I, pages 23–24; Shock; Unconscious

● **Heat cramps:** see Overexposure: Heat and Cold (heat injuries)

● **Heat exhaustion:** see Overexposure: Heat and Cold (heat injuries)

● **Heat rash:** see Rashes (heat rash)

● **Heatstroke:** see Part I, page 31; Overexposure: Heat and Cold (heat injuries); Unconscious

● **Hematoma:** see Bruises

● **Heroin, abuse:** see Drug Abuse

● **Hip injury:** see Broken Bones and Spinal Injuries; Dislocations

● **Hives:** see Rashes (hives); Shock (shock from reaction to insect sting)

● **Hornet stings:** see Bites and Stings (insect stings)

● **Hospitals:** see Part I, pages 43 – 45

● **Hyperventilation:** see Unconscious (hyperventilation)

● **Hypothermia:** see Part I, page 31; Overexposure: Heat and Cold (cold injuries)

● **Identification, emergency medical:** see Part I, page 6

● **Indigestion:** see Abdominal Pain; Diarrhea; Heart Attack

Influenza: see Abdominal Pain; Chills; Diarrhea

Inner ear disturbance: see Unconscious (vertigo)

Insect stings: see Rashes (bites and stings); Shock (shock from reaction to insect sting); Unconscious

Insulin shock: see Shock (insulin shock); Unconscious

Internal bleeding: see Bleeding (internal bleeding)

Internal injury: see Wounds (closed wounds)

Itching: see Poisons (plant irritations); Rashes; Shock (shock from reaction to insect sting)

Jellyfish stings: see Bites and Stings (marine life)

Joint pains: see Broken Bones and Spinal Injuries; Dislocations; Muscle aches and Pains; Sprains

Kerosene, inhalant: see Drug Abuse

Knee injury: see Broken Bones and Spinal Injuries; Dislocations; Sprains

Knife wounds: see Wounds (puncture wounds)

Lacerations: see Wounds

Lead poisoning: see Poisons (food poisoning)

Leg injury: see Broken Bones and Spinal Injuries; Muscle Aches and Pains

● **Librium, abuse:** see Drug Abuse

Ligament pain: see Sprains

● **Lighter fluid, inhalant:** see Drug Abuse

Lightning striking: see Electric Shock

● **Lockjaw:** see Bites and Stings (animal); Minor Injuries; Wounds

Loose bowels: see Diarrhea

● **LSD, abuse:** see Drug Abuse

LUMPS AND BUMPS

Lumps and bumps are common injuries. Any bump on the head resulting from an injury may be serious and require medical attention.

AS SOON AS INJURY OCCURS

WHAT TO DO (1) Apply cold compresses or ice pack to the affected area to decrease swelling and alleviate pain.

(2) Seek medical attention promptly for a lump on the head if there is bleeding from the ears, nose or mouth, unconsciousness, a change in pulse, severe headache, difficulty in breathing, convulsions, severe vomiting, unequal eye pupils, slurred speech, a generally poor appearance or a personality change.

(3) If a bump is a result of a head injury, check or awaken victim every one-half hour for the first two hours, every two hours for the next 24 hours, every four hours for the second 24-hour period and every eight hours for the third 24-hour period. By doing this, you are checking to be sure that the victim has not become unconscious.

(4) Seek medical attention for any severe lump or bump on any part of the body.

See Also: Broken Bones and Spinal Injuries; Bruises; Eye Injuries (blunt injuries); Headache; Head Injuries; Unconscious

● **Marijuana, abuse:** see Drug Abuse

● **Measles:** see Rashes (diseases)

● **Meningitis:** see Headaches; Rashes

● **Menstrual cramps:** see Abdominal Pain; Miscarriage; Pregnancy, Danger Signs

● **Mescaline, abuse:** see Drug Abuse

- **Methedrine, abuse:** see Drug Abuse
- **Middle ear infection:** see Ear Injuries and Earaches
- **Migraine headaches:** see Headaches

MINOR INJURIES

BLISTERS

Blisters are usually caused by clothing (such as shoes) or equipment repeatedly rubbing against the skin.

WHAT TO DO
(1) If blister is small and unopened, and will receive no further irritation, cover it with a sterile gauze pad and bandage in place. The fluid in the blister will eventually be absorbed by the skin and it will heal itself.

(2) If the blister accidentally breaks, exposing raw skin, wash area gently with soap and water and cover with a sterile bandage. The skin will regrow its outer layers.

(3) *Do not* open a blister that was caused by a burn.

(4) If the blister is large and likely to be broken by routine activity, you should seek medical attention for treatment. Only if medical attention is not readily available should you try to open the blister.

(5) Gently clean the area with soap and water. Sterilize a needle by holding it over an open flame. Puncture the lower edge of the blister with the needle. Press blister gently to force out fluid. Cover area with a sterile bandage.

(6) Always look for signs of infection such as redness, pus or red streaks leading from the wound. Seek medical attention promptly if these symptoms appear.

FISHHOOK INJURY

Catching a fishhook in the body is a common injury. If the fishhook goes deep enough so that the barb is embedded in the skin, it is best to have a doctor remove it. If a doctor is not readily available, the hooks should be removed.

BEWARE *Never* remove a fishhook caught in the eye or face.

WHAT TO DO (1) If only the point of the hook, and not the barb, entered the skin, remove the hook by backing it out.
(2) If the hook is embedded in the skin, push the hook through the skin until the barb comes out.
(3) Cut the hook with pliers, clippers, etc., at either the barb or the shank of the hook. Remove the part remaining.
(4) Clean the wound with soap and water and cover with a bandage. *(Continued on next page.)*

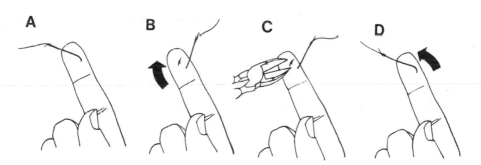

A. *Fishhook embedded beyond the barb in the tip of the finger.*
B. *Push hook through the skin until the barb comes out.*
C. *Cut the hook with pliers, etc., at the barb (as illustrated) or at the shank.*
D. *Carefully remove the remaining part of the hook.*

(5) Seek medical attention as soon as possible. In such injuries there is always the possibility of infection, particularly tetanus.

INJURED FINGERTIP
(Hammer, slammed door, etc.)

Injuries to the fingertip resulting from a hammer, slammed door, etc., are extremely painful. Small blood vessels under the fingernail may break, causing a blood clot to form. Within several days, the nail turns black and becomes very painful from the pressure of the blood clot.

Note:

It is recommended that a doctor remove the blood clot. However, if medical assistance is not available for a few days and the pain is severe, you can do this yourself by following these directions.

WHAT TO DO
(1) If the blood clot is deep beneath the fingernail, seek medical attention for draining.

(2) If the blood clot is close to the tip of the finger, it may be drained.

(3) Sterilize a needle or paper clip (straightened out) in boiling water for about five minutes or hold over an open flame until red hot.

(4) Gently puncture the blood clot to allow draining by inserting the needlepoint under the fingernail into the clot area. You may have to do this several times in order to break the blood clot.

(5) Cover with a sterile bandage.

(6) The fingernail should not be pulled off if it becomes loose. Keep the nail in place with a Band-Aid® to allow the new fingernail to push off the old one.

(7) If the injury is severe, medical attention is recommended for a possible broken bone.

SPLINTERS

WHAT TO DO
(1) Wash your hands and the victim's skin around the splinter with soap and water.
(2) Place a sewing needle and tweezers in boiling water for about five minutes or hold over an open flame to sterilize.
(3) If the splinter is sticking out of the skin, gently pull the splinter out with the tweezers at the same angle in which it entered.
(4) If the splinter is not deeply lodged below the skin and is clearly visible, gently loosen the skin around the splinter with the needle and carefully remove the splinter with the tweezers at the same angle in which it entered.
(5) Squeeze the wound gently to allow slight bleeding to wash out germs.
(6) If splinter breaks off in the skin or is deeply lodged, seek medical attention for removal and possible tetanus shot.
(7) After the splinter is removed, wash the area with soap and water and apply a Band-Aid®.
(8) Watch for any signs of infection such as redness, pus or red streaks leading up the body from the wound.
See Also: Bleeding; Broken Bones and Spinal Injuries; Ear Injuries and Earaches; Eye Injuries; Head Injuries; Wounds

MISCARRIAGE

A miscarriage is the loss of a fetus before the twentieth week of pregnancy. Miscarriages are common and occur in approximately 10 percent of pregnancies.

The first signs of a possible miscarriage are usually bleeding followed by lower abdominal cramping. Although vaginal bleeding and/or cramping do not always result in a miscarriage, if either of these symptoms appear your doctor should be notified immediately. If heavy or continuous bleeding occurs, seek medical attention immediately, preferably at the nearest hospital emergency room.

Until the doctor is notified and can give specific instructions, the woman should rest in bed. If any material resembling the fetus (tissue, unusual-looking clots, etc.) is passed from the vagina, it should be saved (preferably in a container in the refrigerator) for inspection by the doctor.

See Also: Abdominal Pain; Childbirth, Emergency; Pregnancy, Danger Signs

MUSCLE ACHES AND PAINS

Pain in the muscles is common and usually not serious. These pains are often caused by tension, infections, fatigue (particularly in children) and overexercising. (See also Sprains; Strains.) Gently massaging the area, applying heat such as a warm bath or warm wet compresses and resting are often helpful in relieving the pain. Stretching exercises begun slowly also may be helpful. Any pain that is severe or prolonged needs medical attention.

Muscle cramps can be particularly painful and often occur in the middle of the night. They usually result from fatigue. Muscle cramps often occur in the foot, the calf of the leg and the thigh. Massaging the area to relax the muscle is usually effective, because it stimulates local circulation.

If the cramp is in the foot, turn the toes up toward your body and bend the foot back. If the cramp is in the calf of the leg, stand up with most of your weight on the unaffected leg and massage the cramp. For a cramp in the thigh, lie down while massaging the area. Heat is often helpful.

Cramps in the legs and thighs often occur during pregnancy. The treatment is the same as described for muscle cramps. Also be sure to get plenty of rest.

See Also: Bites and Stings (spider bites); Broken Bones and Spinal Injuries; Bruises; Dislocations; Overexposure: Heat and Cold (heat exhaustion); Poisons (food); Sprains; Strains

● **Mushroom poisoning:** see Poisons (food poisoning)

● **Nail polish, inhalant:** see Drug Abuse

● **Narcotics, abuse:** see Drug Abuse

● **Nausea:** see Part I, page 10; Abdominal Pain; Diarrhea; Heart Attack; Overexposure: Heat and Cold; Poisons; Pregnancy, Danger Signs; Vomiting

● **Neck Injury:** see Part I, pages 24 – 27; Broken Bones and Spinal Injuries; Headaches; Head Injuries

● **Nerve injury:** see Broken Bones and Spinal Injuries; Head Injuries; Stroke

● **Nosebleeds:** see Bleeding (nosebleeds)

● **Opium, abuse:** see Drug Abuse

● **Overdose symptoms:** see Drug Abuse

● **Overexertion:** see Muscle Aches and Pains

OVEREXPOSURE: HEAT AND COLD

ABCs

With all serious injuries, check and maintain an open Airway. Restore Breathing and Circulation if necessary. *(Continued on next page.)*

Tilt head backward to maintain an open airway.

HEAT INJURIES

Heatstroke (Sunstroke)

Heatstroke is a life-threatening emergency. It is a disturbance in the body's heat-regulating system caused by extremely high body temperature due to exposure to heat.

SYMPTOMS

(1) Body temperature extremely high (often 106°F or higher).
(2) Skin is red, hot and dry. Sweating is absent.
(3) Rapid and strong pulse.
(4) Possible unconsciousness or confusion.
(5) Any one or all of the above may be present.

If body temperature reaches 105°F:

IMMEDIATE TREATMENT

(1) Undress victim and put him into a tub of cold water (not iced) if possible. Otherwise, spray victim with hose, sponge bare skin with cool water or rubbing alcohol, or apply cold packs to victim's body.
(2) Continue treatment until body temperature is lowered to 101° or 102°F.
(3) Do not overchill. Check temperature constantly.
(4) Dry off victim once temperature is lowered.
(5) Seek medical attention promptly, preferably at the nearest hospital emergency room.

CONTINUED CARE

(1) Place victim in front of fan or air conditioner to continue cooling.
(2) If body temperature rises again, repeat cooling process.
(3) *Do not* give victim alcoholic beverages or stimulants such as coffee or tea.

Heat Exhaustion

Heat exhaustion can occur after prolonged exposure to high temperatures and high humidity.

SYMPTOMS

(1) Body temperature normal or slightly above normal.
(2) Skin is pale and clammy.
(3) Heavy sweating.
(4) Tiredness, weakness.
(5) Dizziness.
(6) Headache.
(7) Nausea.
(8) Possible muscle cramps.
(9) Possible vomiting.
(10) Possible fainting.
(11) Any one or all of the above may be present.

WHAT TO DO

(1) Move victim into shade or to a cooler area.
(2) Have victim lie down.
(3) Raise victim's feet 8 to 12 inches.
(4) Loosen victim's clothing.
(5) If victim is not vomiting, give clear juice or sips of cool salt water (1 teaspoon of salt per glass). Give victim half a glass of liquid every 15 minutes for one hour. Stop fluids if vomiting occurs.
(6) Place cool wet cloths on victim's forehead and body.
(7) Use a fan to cool victim or, if possible, remove victim to an air-conditioned room.
(8) If symptoms are severe, become worse or last longer than an hour, seek medical attention promptly.

Heat Cramps

Heat cramps are muscle pains and spasms caused by a loss of salt from the body due to heavy sweating. Strenuous physical activity in hot temperatures can lead to heat cramps. Usually the muscles of the stomach and legs are affected first. Heat cramps may also be a symptom of heat exhaustion.

SYMPTOMS
(1) Painful muscle cramping and spasms.
(2) Heavy sweating.
(3) Possible convulsions.
(4) Any one or all of the above may be present.

WHAT TO DO
(1) Have victim sit quietly in a cool place.
(2) Apply firm hand pressure to affected area or gently massage victim's cramped muscles.
(3) If victim is not vomiting, give clear juice or sips of cool salt water (1 teaspoon of salt per glass). Give victim half a glass of liquid every 15 minutes for one hour.
(4) Medical attention is needed if available because of other possible complications.

Sunburn

Sunburn is usually a first-degree burn of the skin resulting from overexposure to the sun. Prolonged exposure can lead to a second-degree burn.

SYMPTOMS
(1) Redness.
(2) Pain.
(3) Mild swelling.
(4) Blisters and considerable swelling in severe cases.
(5) Any one or all of the above may be present.

WHAT TO DO
(1) Put cold water on sunburned area.
(2) If sunburn is severe, submerge sunburned area under cold water until pain is relieved. It is also helpful to place cold wet cloths on burned area. Do not rub the skin.
(3) Elevate severely sunburned arms or legs.
(4) If possible, put a dry sterile bandage on severely sunburned area.

(5) Seek medical attention for severe sunburn. *Do not* break blisters or put ointments, sprays, antiseptic medications or home remedies on severe sunburns.

COLD INJURIES

Frostbite

Frostbite is the freezing of parts of the body due to exposure to very low temperatures. Frostbite occurs when ice crystals form in the fluid in the cells of the skin and tissues. The toes, fingers, nose, and ears are affected most often.

SYMPTOMS

(1) In the earliest stages skin appears red. Pain is often present.
(2) As frostbite develops, skin becomes white or grayish yellow and appears and feels waxy and firm.
(3) Skin feels very cold and numb.
(4) Pain disappears.
(5) Possible blisters.
(6) Often victim is not aware he has frostbite until someone else notices his symptoms.
(7) Any one or all of the above may be present.

IMMEDIATE TREATMENT

(1) While outside, cover the frozen part with extra clothing or a warm cloth. If hand or fingers are frostbitten, put hand under armpit next to body for additional warmth.
(2) *Do not* rub frostbitten part with snow or anything else.
(3) Bring victim inside promptly.
(4) Frostbitten area must be rewarmed rapidly. Put victim's frostbitten part in *warm* (not hot) water that is between 100° and 104°F. Test water with thermometer or by pouring water over the inside of your arm.
(5) If warm water is not available, gently wrap

frostbitten part in blankets or other warm materials.

(6) *Do not* use heat lamps, hot water bottles or heating pads.

(7) *Do not* allow victim to place frostbitten part near a hot stove or radiator. Frostbitten parts may become burned before feeling recurs.

(8) *Do not* break blisters.

(9) Stop warming process when skin becomes pink and/or feeling begins to come back.

(10) Seek medical attention promptly

CONTINUED CARE

(1) Give victim warm drinks such as tea, coffee or soup.

(2) *Do not* give alcoholic beverages.

(3) Have victim exercise fingers or toes as soon as they are warmed.

(4) *Do not* allow victim with frostbitten feet or toes to walk. This may cause further damage to frostbitten part.

(5) Put sterile gauze between frostbitten fingers or toes to keep them separated.

(6) Keep frostbitten parts elevated, if possible.

(7) Take extreme care that frostbitten area is not refrozen after it has thawed.

Chilling and Freezing of Entire Body (Hypothermia)

SYMPTOMS

(1) Shivering.

(2) Numbness.

(3) Drowsiness, sleepiness.

(4) Muscle weakness.

(5) Low body temperature.

(6) Unconsciousness if entire body is severely chilled or frozen.

(7) Any one or all of the above may be present.

IMMEDIATE
TREATMENT
(1) Maintain an open airway and restore breathing if necessary.
(2) Bring victim into a warm room as soon as possible.
(3) Remove wet clothes.
(4) Wrap victim in warm blankets, towels, additional clothing, sheets, etc.
(5) Seek medical attention promptly.

CONTINUED
CARE
(1) If victim is conscious, give him comfortably warm drinks such as coffee, tea or soup.
(2) *Do not* give victim alcoholic beverages.
(3) See treatment and care for Frostbite on pages 187–88.

Mild Chilling

For mild chilling put victim in a warm room and wrap in warm blankets. Give victim warm drinks such as coffee, tea or soup. *Do not* give victim alcoholic beverages.
See Also: Part I, page 31; Burns; Convulsions; Drowning; Ear Injuries and Earaches (frostbite); Fever; Unconscious

● **Paint:** see Poisons (food poisoning)

● **Paint, inhalant:** see Drug Abuse

● **Paralysis:** see Broken Bones and Spinal Injuries; Head Injuries; Stroke

● **Paramedics:** see Part I, pages 43 – 45

● **Passed out:** see Unconscious

● **Pelvic injury:** see Broken Bones and Spinal Injuries

● **Pep pills, abuse:** see Drug Abuse

● **Period, menstrual:** see Abdominal Pains

● **Pink eye:** see Eye Injuries (pink eye)

● **Pneumonia:** see Chills

● **Poison ivy:** see Poisons (plant irritations); Rashes (poisonous rashes)

Poison oak: see Poisons (plant irritations); Rashes (poisonous rashes)

POISONS

ABCs

With all serious injuries maintain an open Airway. Restore Breathing and Circulation if necessary.

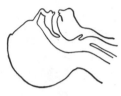

Tilt head backward to maintain an open airway.

POISONING FROM HOUSEHOLD PRODUCTS THAT ARE SWALLOWED

It is extremely important to call a Poison Control Center (if available), a hospital emergency room, a doctor or paramedics for instructions if someone has swallowed a poison. When calling, be sure to give the following information:

(1) Victim's age.
(2) Name of the poison.
(3) How much poison was swallowed.
(4) When poison was swallowed.
(5) Whether or not the victim has vomited.
(6) How much time it will take to get the victim to a medical facility.

Emergency treatment for victims of swallowed poisons consists of:

(1) Diluting the poison with water or milk as

quickly as possible. *Do not* give fruit juice or vinegar to neutralize the poison.

(2) Getting the poison out of the victim by induced vomiting (on medical advice only— preferably from the staff at a Poison Control Center).

(3) Seeking prompt medical attention.

BEWARE

Never give liquids to dilute the poison or induce vomiting if the victim is unconscious or is having convulsions. Also, *do not induce vomiting if* you do not know what the victim has swallowed.

Do not induce vomiting if the victim has swallowed:

(1) A strong ACID such as toilet bowl cleaner, rust removers, chlorine bleach, dishwasher detergent or clinitest tablets.

(2) PETROLEUM PRODUCTS such as kerosene, gasoline, furniture polish, charcoal lighter fluid or paint thinner.

Give water, not milk, with these products.

Strong acids and alkalis, if vomited, may cause further damage to the throat and esophagus. Petroleum products, if vomited, can be sucked into the lungs and cause a chemical pneumonia. It is important to note, however, that Poison Control Centers may recommend induced vomiting for some of the above-mentioned products (particularly the petroleum products) because of other, more harmful effects to the body.

Always follow the instructions of the Poison Control Center.

If the victim vomits, whether induced or spontaneous, keep the victim's face down with head lower than the rest of his body so that he will not choke on the vomit. Place a small child face down across your knees (spanking position). *Be sure* to take the poison container and any vomited material to the hospital for inspection.

Note:

Antidotes on labels of poisonous substances are not always correct, particularly if the container is old. It is always best to consult a Poison Control Center if possible.

If the victim is *not* breathing:

IMMEDIATE TREATMENT

(1) Maintain an open airway.
(2) Restore breathing. (See Electric Shock, Immediate Treatment, on pages 151–55.)
(3) Seek medical attention immediately. Call paramedics, ambulance, fire department or other rescue personnel for transportation to the hospital.
(4) Take the poison container and any vomited material to the hospital with the victim.

If the victim is *unconscious* or *having convulsions:*

IMMEDIATE TREATMENT

(1) Maintain an open airway if possible. Restore breathing if necessary.
(2) Loosen tight clothing around the victim's neck and waist.
(3) Seek medical attention immediately. Call paramedics, ambulance, fire department or other rescue personnel for transportation to the hospital. Victim should be transported lying on his side or stomach.
(4) Take the poison container and any vomited material to the hospital with the victim.
(5) *Do not* give any fluids to the victim.
(6) *Do not* try to induce vomiting. If the victim vomits on his own, turn his head to the side so that he will not choke on the vomit.

If the victim is conscious:

IMMEDIATE TREATMENT

(1) Immediately give the victim at least one 8-ounce glass of water or milk (give only water with gasoline products) to dilute the poison.

Do not give fruit juice, vinegar, carbonated drinks or alcohol to neutralize the poison.

(2) Have someone else (if possible) call the Poison Control Center, hospital emergency room or doctor for further instructions while you continue to care for the victim.

(3) Induce vomiting *only* if told to do so by one of the above listed medical personnel. If no medical advice is readily available, induce vomiting only if the swallowed poison is *not* an acid, alkali, or petroleum product. Vomiting may be induced by giving an adult (over 12 years of age unless low weight) 2 tablespoons of Syrup of Ipecac; a child, 1 tablespoon of Syrup of Ipecac; an infant under 1 year of age, 2 teaspoons. Follow with one to two glasses of water or milk. If vomiting does not occur within 15 to 20 minutes repeat dosage of Ipecac *only* once.

(4) *Do not* give mustard or table salt to the victim to induce vomiting.

(5) If Syrup of Ipecac is not available, induce vomiting by tickling the back of the victim's throat with your finger or a spoon.

(6) If vomiting does not occur, seek medical attention immediately.

(7) If vomiting occurs, keep the victim face down with his head lower than the rest of his body so that he will not choke on the vomit. Place a small child face down across your knees.

(8) Seek medical attention immediately. Take the poison container and any vomited material to the hospital with the victim.

POISONING FROM SMOKE, CHEMICAL OR GAS FUMES

BEWARE

Be extremely cautious when rescuing a victim from an area filled with smoke, chemical or gas fumes. It is best not to attempt a rescue alone. Before entering the area, rapidly inhale and exhale two or three times; then take a deep breath and hold it. Remain close to the ground (crawl) while entering and rescuing the victim so that you will not inhale hot air or fumes. If the area is extremely hot or heavy with fumes, it is best for the rescuer to have an independent air supply. Do nothing but rescue the victim.

IMMEDIATE TREATMENT

(1) Get the victim into fresh air immediately.
(2) Maintain an open airway. Restore breathing and circulation if necessary.
(3) Loosen tight clothing around the victim's neck and waist.
(4) Seek medical attention immediately even if the victim seems to recover completely or partially. Call paramedics, an ambulance or other trained rescue personnel and inform medics of the need for oxygen.

SKIN POISONING

See Burns, Chemical on pages 105–06.

PLANT IRRITATIONS (poison ivy, poison oak and poison sumac)

An oily substance on the plants causes the irritation.

SYMPTOMS

(1) Redness of the skin.
(2) Blisters.
(3) Itching.
(4) Headache.
(5) Fever.

Poison Ivy: *May grow as a plant, bush or vine. Leaf has three shiny leaflets.*

WHAT TO DO (1) As soon as possible, remove clothes and thoroughly wash the affected area with soap and water.

(2) Sponge the affected area with rubbing alcohol.

(3) Calamine lotion may be applied to relieve itching. *(Continued on next page.)*

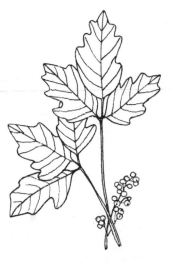

Poison Oak: *May grow as a bush or vine. Leaf has three leaflets.*

(4) Wash clothes thoroughly.
(5) Seek medical attention if the reaction is severe, particulary around the face or genitals.

Poison Sumac: *May grow as a bush or tree. Leaf consists of rows of two leaflets opposite each other plus leaflet at top. Leaflets are pointed at both ends.*

FOOD POISONING

Suspect food poisoning if several people become ill with similar symptoms at approximately the same time after eating the same food. Also suspect food poisoning if one person becomes ill after eating food no one else ate.

Botulism

Botulism most often occurs after eating improperly home-canned foods. Botulism is a very serious form of food poisoning and is often fatal. It is a medical emergency.

SYMPTOMS   Symptoms usually appear within 12 to 36 hours.

(1) Dizziness.
(2) Headache.

(3) Blurred and/or double vision.
(4) Muscle weakness.
(5) Difficulty in swallowing.
(6) Difficulty in talking.
(7) Difficulty in breathing.

IMMEDIATE TREATMENT Seek medical attention immediately, preferably at the nearest hospital emergency room.

Mushroom Poisoning

Mushroom poisoning occurs after eating certain mushrooms found growing wild.

SYMPTOMS Symptoms appear within minutes to 24 hours, depending on the type and amount of mushrooms eaten. Symptoms may vary according to the type of mushrooms.

(1) Abdominal pain.
(2) Diarrhea (may contain blood).
(3) Vomiting (may contain blood).
(4) Difficulty in breathing.
(5) Sweating.
(6) Salivation.
(7) Tears.
(8) Dizziness.

IMMEDIATE TREATMENT
(1) Call the Poison Control Center, hospital emergency room or doctor for instructions.
(2) Keep the victim resting in a quiet place.
(3) If medical advice is not readily available, induce vomiting if vomiting has not already occurred. See Immediate Treatment, number 3, on page 193.
(4) Seek medical attention immediately.

Salmonella Poisoning

Salmonella poisoning usually occurs after eating fresh food that has been contaminated with salmonella bacteria. Foods most commonly affected include eggs, milk, raw meats, raw poultry and raw fish. Salmonella poisoning can be very serious in infants, young children, the elderly and the chronically ill.

SYMPTOMS Symptoms usually appear from six to 24 hours after eating contaminated food.

(1) Abdominal cramps.
(2) Diarrhea.
(3) Fever.
(4) Chills.
(5) Headache.
(6) Vomiting.
(7) Weakness.

WHAT TO DO (1) Keep the victim lying down.
(2) Keep the victim comfortably warm.
(3) After vomiting is over, give the victim warm mild fluids, such as tea, broth or fruit juices.
(4) Seek medical attention promptly.

Staphylococcus Poisoning

Staphylococcus poisoning occurs most often by eating foods that have not been properly refrigerated. The most common foods affected include meats, poultry, eggs, milk, cream-filled bakery goods, tuna and potato salad.

SYMPTOMS Symptoms usually appear two to six hours after contaminated food has been eaten.

(1) Abdominal cramps.
(2) Nausea.
(3) Vomiting.
(4) Diarrhea.

WHAT TO DO (1) Keep the victim resting, preferably in bed.
(2) *After* the vomiting is over, give the victim warm mild fluids such as tea, broth or fruit juices.

(3) It is best to seek medical attention, particularly if the symptoms are severe or persist.

LEAD POISONING

Lead poisoning most often occurs in young children who nibble on paint chips, plaster, putty and other substances containing lead.

SYMPTOMS
(1) Vomiting.
(2) Weakness.
(3) Fatigue.
(4) Irritability.
(5) Fever.
(6) Paleness.
(7) Convulsions.

Brain damage may result from prolonged exposure to lead poisoning.

It is extremely important to seek medical attention as soon as lead poisoning is suspected.

See Also: Abdominal Pains; Bites and Stings; Burns (chemical burns); Convulsions: Diarrhea; Drug Abuse; Rashes; Unconscious

● **Poison sumac:** see Poisons (plant irritations); Rashes (poisonous rashes)

● **Portuguese man-of-war stings:** see Bites and Stings (marine life)

PREGNANCY, DANGER SIGNS

Certain symptoms during pregnancy should be reported immediately to a doctor. They may or may not indicate a serious condition, but only a doctor can evaluate the situation. The symptoms to report immediately include:

(1) *Any* vaginal bleeding.
(2) Stomach pain or cramps.

(3) Persistent vomiting.
(4) Severe, persistent headaches.
(5) Swelling of the face or fingers.
(6) Blurring or dimness of vision.
(7) Chills and fever.
(8) Sudden leaking of water from the vagina.
(9) Convulsions.

See Also: Childbirth, Emergency; Miscarriage

● **Pressure points:** see Part I, pages 27 – 31; Bleeding

● **Prickly heat:** see Rashes (heat rash)

● **Psilocybin, abuse:** see Drug Abuse

● **Pulse rate, how to take:** see Part I, page 9

● **Puncture wounds:** see Wounds (puncture wounds)

● **Quaaludes, abuse:** see Drug Abuse

● **Rabies:** see Bites and Stings (animal)

RASHES

Skin rashes occur for many reasons. They may be due to allergic reactions, fever or heat, infectious diseases or other causes. Some rashes may indicate a serious problem. Medical attention should always be sought if blue, purple or blood-red spots appear (these may mean bleeding in and under the skin); the rash becomes worse; signs of infection such as pus or red streaks occur; itching is severe; or if other symptoms are present.

HEAT RASH

A common rash is heat rash (also called prickly heat). In heat rash the body's sweat ducts are blocked. This rash is caused by high body temperatures due to fever or hot humid weather. The area affected is covered with tiny red pinpoints. Treatment consists of avoiding extreme heat.

Dusting powders and soothing lotions are also helpful. Light, dry and loose clothing should be worn in hot weather. Heat rash usually disappears in a cool environment. If heat rash persists, a doctor should be consulted.

HIVES

Hives are an allergic reaction to various substances characterized by large or small irregularly shaped and sized bumpy swellings that cause stinging, burning and itching. Animal hairs, feathers, plants, fabrics, dyes and viral infections may cause hives. Food is a common offender, particularly chocolate, nuts, berries and seafood. If hives have occurred before, follow previous instructions of the doctor. If hives persist, see your doctor. For first attacks of hives, it is best to seek medical attention. If other symptoms are present, such as difficulty in breathing or swallowing, seek medical attention promptly.

DRUG RASH

A skin reaction may appear with any medication although these rashes are more likely to appear with the use of powerful drugs such as barbiturates, tranquilizers and antibiotics. If a rash appears while on a medication, call a doctor immediately to see if a rash is to be expected from the illness for which the medication was prescribed, or if it is a reaction to the drug.

BITES AND STINGS

Rashes may appear after insect stings, tick bites, brown recluse spider bites and rat bites. Rashes that result from bites and stings should be seen by a doctor. Some may rapidly lead to breathing difficulties. (See Bites and Stings.)

POISONOUS RASHES

Contact with plants often produces a rash in sensitive persons. The most common offenders are poison ivy, poison oak, and poison sumac. (See Poisons, Plant Irritations.)

DISEASES

Rashes are present with many infectious diseases. Among these are chicken pox, German measles (three day), Rocky Mountain spotted fever, smallpox, scarlet fever, certain forms of meningitis, roseola infantum, and infectious mononucleosis.

RASHES IN INFANTS

Infants often have rashes. The most common is diaper rash. It is not dangerous but can cause a lot of discomfort. Diaper rash usually is an ammonia burn which occurs when bacteria acts upon passed urine that stays on the skin for prolonged periods and breaks down the urine into ammonia. Diaper rash may also be caused by fungi found in the infant's stools. Thorough skin cleansing followed by drying will help. *Very* absorbent, dry diapers should be used and changed frequently. Various ointments are available, but it is best to ask a doctor for specific instructions.

A common rash to newborns appears during the early weeks of life. It may appear anywhere on the body. It often moves from one place to another. The affected area should be kept clean and dry. It is always a good idea to report all rashes on an infant to a doctor.

Rashes seen on infants are also caused by food allergies and by contact with substances such as clothes washed in strong detergents, rubber in pants, skin care products and soap left behind the ears. These rashes should also be reported to a doctor.

See Also: Bites and Stings; Poisons (plant irritations)

● **Rattlesnake bites:** see Bites and Stings (snakes)
● **Rocky Mountain Spotted Fever:** see Rashes (diseases)
● **Runs:** see Diarrhea
● **Ruptured eardrum:** see Ear Injuries and Earaches
● **Salmonella poisoning:** see Poisons (food poisoning)
● **Scalding:** see Burns
● **Scalp cuts:** see Head Injuries (cuts of the scalp)
● **Scarlet fever:** see Rashes (diseases)
● **Scorpion bites:** see Bites and Stings (scorpions)
● **Scratches:** see Wounds (scrapes and scratches)
● **Sedative, abuse:** see Drug Abuse
● **Seizures:** see Convulsions (seizures)
● **Self-destruction:** see Suicide, Threatened
● **Setting broken bones:** see Broken Bones and Spinal Injuries; Dislocations
● **Severed limbs:** see Part I, page 32
● **Shakes:** see Chills; Overexposure: Heat and Cold
● **Shivering:** see Chills; Overexposure: Heat and Cold (cold injuries)

SHOCK

ABCs

With all serious injuries, maintain an open Airway. Restore Breathing and Circulation if necessary.

(Continued on next page.)

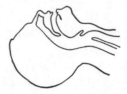

Tilt head backward to maintain an open airway.

SHOCK DUE TO INJURY (Traumatic)

Traumatic shock is a life-threatening situation in which the body's vital functions are seriously threatened by insufficient blood, or oxygen in the blood, reaching the body tissues. Injuries that result in loss of blood, loss of body fluid, too little oxygen reaching the lungs, loss of nervous control, severe infections or heart problems can lead to shock. Shock is a medical condition secondary to serious illness or injury.

SYMPTOMS

(1) Pale or bluish and cool skin.
(2) Moist and clammy skin.
(3) Overall weakness.
(4) Rapid (over 100 beats per minute) and weak pulse.
(5) Rate of breathing increased; breathing may be shallow and irregular, or deep sighing.
(6) Restlessness, anxiety.
(7) Unusual thirst.
(8) Vomiting.
(9) Dull, sunken look to the eyes; pupils widely dilated.
(10) Unresponsiveness.
(11) Skin may become blotchy or streaked.
(12) Possible unconsciousness in severe cases.
(13) Any one or all of the above may be present.

IMMEDIATE TREATMENT

(1) Maintain an open airway.
(2) Treat cause of shock such as breathing difficulties, bleeding, severe pain, etc.
(3) Keep victim lying down.
(4) Cover victim only enough to prevent loss of body heat. Keep patient comfortable.
(5) Seek medical attention promptly.

CONTINUED CARE

(1) *Do not* move the victim if he has head, neck or back injuries unless the victim is in danger of further injury. Maintain an open airway.
(2) If the victim has suffered an injury and shows any of the following symptoms, such as a pale face, clammy skin, *obvious* blood loss or bloody vomit, elevate the feet 8 to 12 inches.

If the victim has suffered an injury and has a pale face, clammy skin, obvious *blood loss or bloody vomit, elevate the feet 8 to 12 inches.*

(3) If the victim is experiencing chest pain, has a red face, or has difficulty in breathing, elevate the victim's head and shoulders slightly to make breathing easier. Do not elevate the feet. *(Continued on next page.)*

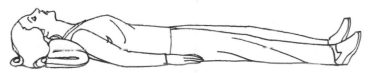

If the victim experiences chest pain, difficulty in breathing or has a red face, elevate victim's head and shoulders slightly to make breathing easier. Do not elevate the feet.

(4) If the victim has no obvious injuries and the reason for shock is unknown, it is best to leave him lying flat.

(5) The victim must be watched very closely for changes in consciousness. If the suggested method (numbers 2, 3 and 4) of placing a victim in shock makes the victim's condition worse or increases the victim's discomfort, discontinue that method and try something else. Again, watch closely to see if the victim becomes better or worse. Often the victim's comfort is the key to what position is correct. *Do not* insist on a certain position if the victim indicates that it makes him uncomfortable.

(6) Check to see that the victim is not getting chilled. Keep him comfortably warm. If possible place a blanket under a victim who is on the ground or on a damp surface.

(7) Look for other injuries such as internal bleeding (see pages 78–79) and broken bones (see pages 80–98) and give first aid to those problems that may decrease the severity of the shock.

(8) *If medical attention is several hours away,* give victim water or a weak solution of salt (1 level teaspoon), baking soda (one-half level teaspoon) mixed with 1 quart of cool water. Give an adult 4 ounces (one-half glass); a child 1 to 12 years 2 ounces; and an infant 1 ounce. Have victim slip slowly over a 15-minute period. Fruit juices may also be given.

   Do not, however, give fluid if victim is unconscious, having convulsions, likely to need surgery, has a brain injury, has a stomach wound, is vomiting or is bleeding from the rectum. Stop fluids if vomiting occurs.

(9) Reassure victim. Gentleness, kindness and understanding play an important role in treating a victim in shock.

(10) If possible, obtain information about the nature of the accident.

SHOCK FROM A REACTION TO INSECT STINGS (Anaphylactic)

Anaphylactic shock is a life-threatening condition resulting from a severe allergic reaction to insect stings.

SYMPTOMS

(1) Weakness.
(2) Coughing and/or wheezing.
(3) Difficulty in breathing.
(4) Severe itching or hives.
(5) Severe swelling in other parts of the body and at the bite site.
(6) Stomach cramps.
(7) Nausea and vomiting.
(8) Anxiety.
(9) Possible bluish tinge to skin.
(10) Collapse.
(11) Possible unconsciousness.
(12) Dizziness.
(13) Any or all of the above may be present.

IMMEDIATE TREATMENT

(1) Maintain an open airway and restore breathing if necessary.
(2) If stung by a honeybee, carefully remove the stinger by gently scraping with a knife blade or fingernail. Removing the stinger reduces the amount of venom entering the body. *Do not* squeeze the stinger while removing it.

If emergency kit for insect stings is *not* available:

(3) If the victim experiences the severe symptoms above, suggesting a severe allergic reaction and the victim is known to have had previous severe reactions to insect stings, the

use of a tourniquet may be necessary. Although not all experts agree on this method, many allergists suggest the use of a tourniquet in severe reactions where the victim's life is at stake. Emergency insect sting kits available only by prescription contain a tourniquet for such cases.

The tourniquet is used only if the sting has just occurred and is on the arm or leg. A rubber tourniquet works best but a strip of cloth, cord, etc., may be used.

Tie the tourniquet 2 to 4 inches above the sting toward the body. *Do not* tie so tightly that the victim's circulation is cut off completely. Loosen the tourniquet about every five minutes until medical assistance is obtained.

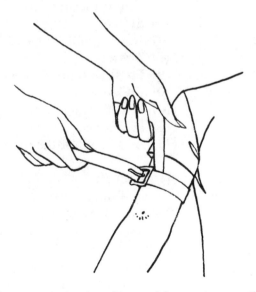

A light constricting band is used for severe *reactions to insect stings (see Insect Stings, Anaphylactic Shock in text) and for rattlesnake, copperhead and cottonmouth (not coral) snake bites. Place the hand 2 to 4 inches above the bite toward the body.* Do not *cut off circulation. You should be able to slip your finger under the band.*

(4) If the victim experiences severe symptoms of an allergic reaction but has no known previous history of severe reactions to insect stings and the sting has just occurred on the arm or leg, apply a light constricting band such as a watchband, belt, etc., 2 to 4 inches above the sting toward the body. The band *should not* be so tight that it cuts off circulation. You should be able to slip your finger under the band. *Do not* remove the band until medical assistance is obtained.

(5) Seek medical attention promptly, preferably at the nearest hospital emergency room.

CONTINUED CARE

(1) Place cold pack or ice wrapped in cloth on sting area.
(2) Keep victim lying down. Turn victim's head to the side if vomiting or position victim on his side.
(3) Keep victim comfortable.

If emergency kit for insect stings *is available:*

IMMEDIATE TREATMENT

(1) Maintain an open airway and restore breathing if necessary.
(2) Remove stinger if stung by a honeybee. (See Immediate Treatment on page 58.)
(3) If victim is unable to administer injection of adrenalin to himself, follow directions in emergency kit.
(4) Seek medical attention promptly, preferably at the nearest hospital emergency room.

CONTINUED CARE

See Continued Care on page 60.

INSULIN SHOCK

Insulin shock occurs when there is too little blood sugar due to the victim taking too much insulin, too little food or overexercising.

SYMPTOMS Symptoms are *completely different* than those of a diabetic coma.

(1) Sudden onset.
(2) Hunger, but no thirst.
(3) Skin is pale and sweaty.
(4) Excited behavior and/or sometimes belligerent behavior.
(5) Breath smells normal, not fruity.
(6) Breathing is normal or shallow.
(7) Mouth and tongue are moist.
(8) No vomiting.
(9) Any one or all of the above may be present.

If victim is *conscious*:

IMMEDIATE
TREATMENT

(1) Give victim food containing sugar such as fruit juice, sweetened drinks (Kool-Aid®), honey, etc., or just sugar in water.
(2) Seek medical attention.

If victim is *unconscious*:

Seek medical attention promptly, preferably at the nearest hospital emergency room.
See Also: Bites and Stings (insects); Bleeding; Convulsions; Drug Abuse; Electric Shock; Heart Attack; Unconscious; Wounds

● **Shortness of breath:** see Asthma; Heart Attack; Poisons; Stroke
● **Shoulder injury:** see Broken Bones and Spinal Injuries; Dislocations; Head Injuries; Sprains
● **Skin, burns:** see Burns
● **Skin irritation:** see Poisons (plant irritations); Rashes
● **Skull injury:** see Head Injuries
● **Sleeping pills, abuse:** see Drug Abuse
● **Sling, how to use:** see Part I, pages 39 – 40
● **Smallpox:** see Rashes (diseases)

● **Smoke inhalation:** see Part I, page 23; Poisons (poisoning from smoke, chemical or gas fumes)

● **Snake bites:** see Bites and Stings (snakes)

● **Sniffing glue:** see Drug Abuse

● **Speed, abuse:** see Drug Abuse

● **Spider bites:** see Bites and Stings (insect bites); Rashes (bites and stings)

● **Spine injury:** see Broken Bones and Spinal Injuries; Head Injuries

● **Spitting up:** see Vomiting

● **Splinters:** see Minor Injuries (splinters); Wounds (puncture wounds)

● **Splints:** see Part I, page 42; Broken Bones and Spinal Injuries

SPRAINS

A sprain is an injury to the ligaments, which support the joints in the body. The ligaments may be stretched or completely torn. A sprain usually results from overextending or twisting a limb beyond its normal range of movement, thus stretching and tearing some of the fibers of the ligament.

SYMPTOMS
(1) Pain upon moving injured part. Pain in the joint.
(2) Swelling of joint.
(3) Tenderness upon touching affected area.
(4) Black and blue discoloration of skin around the area of the injury.

WHAT TO DO
If uncertain as to whether the injury is a sprain or a broken bone, treat as a broken bone. (See Broken Bones on pages 80–98.)

If *ankle* or *knee* is sprained:

(1) Place cold wet packs or a small ice bag wrapped in a cloth over the affected area in-

termittently for the first 12 to 24 hours to decrease local swelling.

(2) Apply supporting bandage, pillow or blanket splint. (See Splinting on pages 83–98.) Loosen support if swelling increases.

(3) Keep injured part elevated above the level of heart.

(4) Keep victim from walking, if possible.

(5) *Do not* use heat or hot water soaks immediately following the injury. They may be applied intermittently 24 hours after the injury.

(6) It is best to seek medical attention to rule out a broken bone. Always seek medical attention if pain or swelling persists.

If *wrist, elbow* or *shoulder* is sprained:

WHAT TO DO
(1) Place injured arm in a sling.

(2) Place cold wet packs or a small ice bag wrapped in a cloth over the affected area.
   Do not use heat or hot water soaks immediately following the injury.

(3) For a wrist injury, apply a supporting bandage. Loosen bandage if swelling increases.

(4) It is best to seek medical attention to rule out a broken bone. Always seek medical attention if pain or swelling persists.
   See Also: Broken Bones and Spinal Injuries; Dislocations; Muscle Aches and Pains

● **Staphylococcus poisoning:** see Poisons (food poisoning)

● **Stimulants, abuse:** see Drug Abuse

● **Stings:** see Bites and Stings; Rashes (bites and stings); Shock (shock from reactions to insect sting); Unconscious

● **Stomachache:** see Abdominal Pain; Diarrhea; Heart Attack; Poisons; Pregnancy, Danger Signs; Vomiting

STRAINS

A strain results from pulling or overexerting a muscle. Back strains are common injuries.

WHAT TO DO
(1) Rest the affected area immediately.
(2) Apply ice or a cold compress to the affected area to decrease swelling.
(3) After 24 hours, apply warm wet compresses to affected area.
(4) If possible, elevate the strained area.
(5) Seek medical attention if pain or swelling is severe.
See Also: Muscle Aches and Pains

STROKE

ABCs
With all serious injuries, check and maintain an open Airway. Restore Breathing and Circulation if necessary.

Tilt head backward to maintain an open airway.

A stroke can be a life-threatening situation. It usually occurs when there is an interruption of the blood supply to part or all of the brain. This interruption in circulation may be caused by the formation of a clot inside an artery supplying blood to the brain, by the narrowing of a blood vessel or by the bursting of an artery within the brain. The brain must receive adequate amounts of blood to function properly. *(Continued on next page.)*

MAJOR STROKE

SYMPTOMS
(1) Sudden headache.
(2) Sudden paralysis, weakness or numbness of the face, arm or leg on the same side of the body. Corner of mouth may droop.
(3) Loss or slurring of speech.
(4) Possible unconsciousness or mental confusion.
(5) Sudden falls.
(6) Impaired vision.
(7) Pupil of the eyes different in size.
(8) Difficulty with breathing, chewing, talking, and/or swallowing.
(9) Loss of bladder and/or bowel control.
(10) Strong, slow pulse.
(11) Any one or all of the above may be present.

IMMEDIATE TREATMENT
(1) Seek medical attention promptly.
(2) Maintain an open airway.
(3) Restore breathing if necessary.

CONTINUED CARE
(1) Place victim on his side so that secretions can drain from his mouth.
(2) Keep victim comfortably warm.
(3) Keep victim quiet.
(4) Apply cold cloths to victim's head.
(5) Reassure and calm victim.
(6) *Do not* give fluids or food to victim. He may vomit or choke on them.

MINOR STROKE

SYMPTOMS
(1) Slight mental confusion.
(2) Slight dizziness.
(3) Minor speech difficulties.
(4) Muscle weakness.

WHAT TO DO
Seek medical attention.

If you are alone:

(1) Call ambulance or doctor immediately.
(2) Lie down on your side so that secretions can drain from your mouth.
(3) Remain quiet until medical help arrives.
(4) Keep comfortably warm, but not too hot.
(5) *Do not* eat or drink anything.
   See Also: Headache; Unconscious

● **Stye:** see Eye Injuries (stye)

SUICIDE, THREATENED

All threats of suicide must be taken seriously. The person threatening to take his life sees his situation as hopeless and sees death as the answer to his problems. Yet most victims need and want help. The victim may very well change his mind if given the chance to do so and it is that chance you want to provide by diverting his immediate thoughts of self-destruction.

If the threat of suicide is unmistakable—that is, the victim is holding a gun, knife, bottle of pills, etc.—you must get the situation under control immediately. Remain calm. Call the police or other professionals trained in dealing with crisis situations. Do not show anger toward the victim or argue with him. Speak in a soft tone and do not make any sudden movement. What you want to do is provide *time*. Encourage the victim to talk, and listen attentively to him. Express interest and concern in what the victim is saying. Once the immediate self-destruction situation is under control, seek professional help for the victim. If possible, go with the victim as he needs to know that someone cares about him.

If the victim is talking about suicide but does not have the means at hand, the immediate situation is not as critical although all suicide talk must be taken seriously. Talk with the victim if he is willing to do so. Listen attentively to him and express interest and concern with his situation. Do not pressure the victim into talking if he does not wish to talk. Always seek professional help when someone expresses a wish to die.

Suicide threats among children are *very* serious, and a child talking of suicide should *not* be left alone until a thorough psychiatric evaluation is done.

There are certain clues and symptoms that may indicate that a person is thinking of suicide. One of these symptoms is severe depression. This is not the same as occasional depressed moods that last only a few days. The victim of severe depression suffers a loss of appetite, loss of sleep and sees no joy or pleasure in his life over a long period of time. Other symptoms include heavy drinking of alcoholic beverages, previous threats or attempts at suicide, a history of suicide in the victim's family, giving away or selling valuable possessions, recent filing of a will or not renewing a rental lease.

See Also: Drug Abuse

● **Sunburn:** see Burns; Overexposure: Heat and Cold (heat injuries)

● **Sunstroke:** see Overexposure: Heat and Cold (heat injuries)

● **Swelling:** see Broken Bones and Spinal Injuries; Dislocations; Sprains

● **Swimming:** see Drowning; Ear Injuries and Earaches (earaches)

● **Tarantula bites:** see Bites and Stings (insect bites)

● **Teeth:** see Dental Emergencies

● **Temperature:** see Overexposure: Heat and Cold

● **Temperature, how to take:** see Fever

● **Tension:** see Headaches; Muscle Aches and Pains

● **Tetanus:** see Bites and Stings (animal); Minor Injuries; Wounds

- **Thermometer, how to read:** see Fever
- **Toothache:** see Dental Emergencies
- **Tourniquet, how to use:** see Bites and Stings; Bleeding; Shock (shock from reaction to insect sting)
- **Toxemia:** see Headaches (headaches in pregnancy)
- **Tranquilizers, abuse:** see Drug Abuse
- **Tubal pregnancy:** see Abdominal Pain (tubal pregnancy)
- **Umbilical cord:** see Childbirth, Emergency

UNCONSCIOUS

There are many causes of unconsciousness. Among these are heart attack, stroke, head injury, bleeding, diabetic coma, insulin shock, poisoning, heatstroke, choking, gas inhalation, severe allergic reaction to insect stings and electric shock.

UNCONSCIOUSNESS

SYMPTOMS

(1) Unresponsive.
(2) Unaware of surroundings.

If unconscious victim is *not* breathing:
(If victim is breathing, see pages 221–22.)

IMMEDIATE TREATMENT— ABCs

I. Open Airway

(1) Lay victim on his back on a firm rigid surface such as the floor or the ground. Loosen tight clothing, particularly around victim's neck.

(2) Quickly clear the mouth and airway of foreign material.

(3) Gently tilt victim's head backward by placing one hand beneath the victim's neck and lifting upward and by placing heel of the

other hand on the victim's forehead and pressing downward as the chin is elevated.

II. Restore Breathing

(1) Keep victim's head tilted backward.

(2) With hand that is placed on victim's forehead, pinch victim's nostrils using the thumb and index finger.

(3) Open your mouth widely and take a deep breath.

(4) Place your mouth tightly around victim's mouth and give four quick breaths. Then continue to blow into his mouth approximately 12 breaths per minute. Quantity is important so provide plenty of air—one breath every five seconds until you see the victim's chest rise. For infants and small children, one light breath every three seconds. (Seconds are counted "one-one thousand, two-one thousand, three-one thousand," etc.)
Note:

(5) If the victim's mouth cannot be used, remove hand under victim's neck and close his mouth. Open your mouth widely and take a deep breath. Place your mouth tightly around the victim's nose and blow into it. After you exhale, remove your hand from the victim's mouth to allow air to escape.

(6) Moderate resistance will be felt with blowing. If chest does not rise, airway is blocked and more airway opening is needed. Place hands under the victim's lower jaw and thrust lower jaw forward so that it juts out.

(7) Watch closely to see when victim's chest rises, and stop blowing when the chest is expanded.

(8) Remove your mouth from victim's mouth

(*Continued on page 220.*)

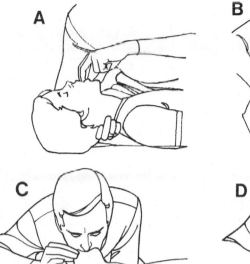

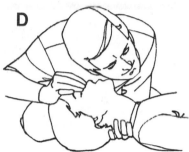

A. Lay victim on his back on a firm, rigid surface. Quickly clear the mouth and airway of foreign material.

B. Tilt the victim's head backward by placing one hand beneath the victim's neck and lifting upward. Place the heel of the other hand on the victim's forehead and press downward as the chin is elevated.

C. With the hand on the victim's forehead, pinch victim's nostrils using your thumb and index finger. Take a deep breath. Place your mouth tightly around the victim's mouth and give four quick breaths. Then give approximately 12 breaths per minute—one breath every five seconds until you see the victim's chest rise.

D. Stop blowing when the victim's chest is expanded. Remove your mouth from the victim's and turn your head toward the victim's chest so that your ear is over the victim's mouth. Listen for air leaving his lungs and watch his chest fall. Repeat breathing procedure.

or nose and turn your head so that your ear is over victim's mouth. Listen for air leaving his lungs. Repeat blowing instructions until victim is breathing well on his own or medical assistance arrives.

III. Restore Circulation

(1) Check neck artery for pulse. Check below left nipple for infant.

(2) If no pulse is present, begin cardiac compressions. This should be done by those professionally trained and *must* be done in conjunction with artificial breathing. (For one rescuer, give 15 compressions [80 per minute]; then two quick breaths. For two rescuers, give five compressions [60 per minute] for every one breath. Repeat until medical assistance arrives.)

IV. Summon Medical Assistance

Call ambulance or paramedics and inform medics of need for oxygen. If this is not possible, take victim to the nearest hospital emergency room. If at all possible, have someone else drive so that you can continue artificial breathing if necessary. Do not stop artificial breathing for more than 15 seconds at any time.

If breathing is restored:

CONTINUED CARE

(1) Keep victim lying down. If cause of unconsciousness is unknown, always suspect a head, neck or back injury and do not move

If victim is unconscious or vomiting, place victim on side with head extended to allow secretions to drain and to prevent choking. Victim's head should be slightly lower than the rest of the body.

victim except to maintain an open airway. If cause of unconsciousness is known, such as a heart attack, diabetic coma, etc., place victim on his side with his head extended to allow secretions to drain and to prevent choking on fluids or vomit. When placed on his side, victim's head should be slightly lower than the rest of his body.

(2) Check for possible cause of unconsciousness such as bleeding, broken bones, head injury, heatstroke, choking, etc., and give first aid. *Do not* waste time treating minor injuries.

(3) Keep victim comfortably warm but not hot.

(4) Do not give unconscious victim anything to eat or drink.

(5) *Do not* leave an unconscious victim alone.

If unconscious victim *is* breathing from onset:

IMMEDIATE TREATMENT

(1) Maintain an open airway.

(2) Loosen tight clothing, particularly around victim's neck.

(3) Keep victim lying down. If cause of unconsciousness is unknown, always suspect a head, neck or back injury and do not move victim except to maintain an open airway. If cause of unconsciousness is known, such as heatstroke, diabetic coma, etc., place victim on his side to allow secretions to drain and to prevent choking on fluids and vomit. When placed on his side, victim's head should be slightly lower than the rest of his body.

(4) Check for possible cause of unconsciousness such as bleeding, broken bones, head injury, etc., and give first aid. *Do not* waste time treating minor injuries.

(5) Seek medical attention promptly, preferably at the nearest hospital emergency room.

CONTINUED CARE

(1) Keep victim comfortably warm but not hot.
(2) *Do not* give unconscious victim anything to eat or drink.
(3) *Do not* leave an unconscious victim alone.

DIABETIC COMA

Diabetic coma occurs when there is too little insulin in the body due to neglected insulin injections, improper diet or infections.

SYMPTOMS

Symptoms are opposite of those of insulin shock.

(1) Gradual onset.
(2) Extreme thirst but no hunger.
(3) Skin is warm, red and dry.
(4) Drowsiness.
(5) Breath smells fruity.
(6) Breathing is deep and rapid.
(7) Mouth and tongue are dry.
(8) Vomiting. Nausea with upper abdominal discomfort.
(9) Frequent urination.
(10) Any one or all of the above may be present.

IMMEDIATE TREATMENT

Seek medical attention promptly, preferably at the nearest hospital emergency room.

FAINTING

Fainting is a brief loss of consciousness due to a reduced blood supply reaching the brain. Recovery usually occurs within a few minutes.

SYMPTOMS

Symptoms may precede or occur during fainting:

(1) Pale, cool and wet skin.
(2) Dizziness.
(3) Nausea.
(4) Any one or all of the above may be present.

To prevent fainting:

WHAT TO DO
(1) Have victim lie down with legs elevated 8 to 12 inches, or have victim sit down and slowly bend his body forward so that his head is between his knees.
(2) Remove any harmful objects out of victim's way.
(3) Calm and reassure victim.

If fainting *has occurred:*

(1) Keep victim lying down. Elevate victim's feet 8 to 12 inches from floor unless head injury is suspected (from falling).
(2) Maintain an open airway.
(3) Loosen tight clothing, particularly around victim's neck.
(4) If victim vomits, place him on his side or turn head sideways to prevent choking on vomit.
(5) Gently bathe victim's face with cool water. *Do not* pour water on victim's face.
(6) Check body parts for swelling or deformity that may have been caused by falling.
(7) *Do not* give victim anything to drink unless he seems fully recovered.
(8) Observe victim after he regains consciousness. Calm and reassure him.
(9) If recovery does not seem complete within a few minutes, seek medical attention.

VERTIGO

Vertigo is a disturbance in the balance mechanism of the inner ear. This disturbance may be caused by an ear infection, an allergy or an injury to the inner ear.

SYMPTOMS
(1) Loss of balance.
(2) Dizziness.
(3) Feeling that everything is spinning around.

(4) Nausea with or without vomiting.

(5) Any one or all of the above may be present.

WHAT TO DO Seek medical attention.

HYPERVENTILATION

Hyperventilation is overbreathing due to a feeling of not getting enough air into the lungs or a tightness in the throat. This excessive breathing is often caused by tension or emotional upset. Feeling out-of-breath results in increased respirations and overbreathing becomes a vicious cycle. As the cycle continues, the level of carbon dioxide in the blood is lowered, causing various distressing symptoms.

SYMPTOMS

(1) Lightheadedness.

(2) Numbness and tingling in the hands, feet and around mouth and lips.

(3) Possible muscle twitching.

(4) May feel difficulty in getting a deep, "satisfying" breath.

(5) Possible convulsions.

(6) Any one or all of the above may be present.

WHAT TO DO

(1) If certain of condition, place a small paper bag loosely over the victim's nose and mouth so he can rebreathe the air and carbon dioxide mixture. Have victim breathe in and out of the bag for four to five minutes. Breathing out (exhaling) should be done slowly.

(2) Seek medical attention if breathing does not return to normal. It is also a good idea to see a doctor to determine the underlying cause of hyperventilation.

See Also: Bites and Stings; Choking; Drug Abuse; Electric Shock; Head Injury; Heart Attack; Poisons; Shock; Stroke

- **Uppers, abuse:** see Drug Abuse
- **Vaginal bleeding:** see Miscarriage; Pregnancy, Danger Signs
- **Valium, abuse:** see Drug Abuse
- **Veins:** see Bleeding
- **Vertigo:** see Unconscious (vertigo)
- **Viper bites:** see Bites and Stings (snakes)
- **Vision impairment:** see Eye Injuries

VOMITING

Vomiting may occur with many conditions. It is particularly common with viral infections of the intestines, excessive eating, excessive drinking of alcoholic beverages and emotional upsets.

Vomiting may be present with more serious conditions such as appendicitis, bowel obstruction, asthma, animal bites, allergic reactions to insect stings, black widow or brown recluse spider bites, marine life bites, scorpion bites, poisonous snake bites, withdrawal from drugs, heart attack, heat exhaustion, shock due to injuries, diabetic coma, food poisoning and head injuries.

Vomiting associated with intestinal viruses, excessive eating or drinking and emotional stress usually does not last a long time. Any vomiting, however, that is severe or lasts longer than a day or two needs medical attention, as dehydration (loss of body fluids) or chemical imbalance (loss of body chemicals) can occur. This is especially true in infants, the elderly or chronically ill persons.

Vomiting can indicate a serious problem. Seek medical attention promptly if vomiting occurs with severe stomach pain or after a recent head injury, or if the vomit contains blood that looks like coffee grounds.

WHAT TO DO In treatment of simple vomiting associated with intestinal upsets, replace lost fluids by frequent sipping of liquids such as carbonated beverages (shake up to eliminate fizz), tea, juice, bouillon, etc. After vomiting has stopped, avoid solid food. Work slowly back to a regular diet.

If victim is unconscious and vomiting, he should be placed on his side with his head extended, as long as he does not have a head, neck or back injury, so that he will not choke on the vomit. A victim with a head injury should have his head turned to the side to prevent choking.

VOMITING IN INFANTS AND YOUNG CHILDREN

Vomiting in infants and children is common. Some of the most common causes include allergy, viral infections (flu), poisoning, car sickness, intestinal obstructions, pneumonia, colic, head injuries, nerves and appendicitis.

In newborns and infants, spitting up food after eating is common and is *not* the same as vomiting. It is usually not serious. Be sure infant does not choke.

Vomiting in infants can be quite serious, particularly if vomited material is expelled with such force that it shoots out of the infant's mouth 1 or 2 feet across the room. This type of vomiting always needs prompt medical attention. This could represent a partial or completely obstructed intestine.

Prolonged vomiting or vomiting with diarrhea can lead to dehydration (loss of body fluids) and also needs prompt medical attention.

Other possibly serious symptoms to watch for in infants and small children include vomit that contains blood, and vomiting with headaches or stomachaches.

WHAT TO DO   In treatment of simple vomiting that accompanies intestinal upsets, etc., the victim should drink fluids and avoid solid foods. Give him small sips (approximately 1 teaspoon) of carbonated beverages (shake up to eliminate fizz), tea or juice (not orange) every 10 to 20 minutes. Gradually increase amount if victim keeps fluids down. Slowly work back to a regular diet once the stomach is settled.

See Also: Abdominal Pain; Bites and Stings; Diarrhea; Drug Abuse; Overexposure:Heat and Cold; Poisons

● **Wasp stings:** see Bites and Stings (insect stings)
● **Whooping cough:** see Croup
● **Withdrawal symptoms:** see Drug Abuse

WOUNDS

ABCs   With all serious injuries, maintain an open Airway. Restore Breathing and Circulation if necessary.

OPEN WOUNDS

An open wound is an injury in which the skin is broken. The objectives in treating an open wound consist of:

(1) Stopping the bleeding.
(2) Preventing contamination and infection.
(3) Preventing or treating for shock if necessary.
(4) Seeking medical attention if the wound is severe or if the victim has not had a tetanus shot within five to seven years.

Cuts (Lacerations)

If bleeding is *severe:*

IMMEDIATE TREATMENT   Use direct pressure. (See Bleeding, Immediate Treatment and Continued Care on pages 73–78). *Do not* clean a large, severe wound or apply any medication.

If bleeding is *not* severe:

WHAT TO DO

(1) Wash your hands thoroughly with soap and water before handling the wound to prevent further contamination of the injury.

(2) If the cut is still bleeding, apply direct pressure over the wound with a sterile or clean cloth.

(3) When the bleeding has stopped, wash the wound thoroughly with soap and water to remove any dirt or other foreign material near the skin's surface. Gentle scrubbing may be necessary. It is very important to remove all dirt, etc., to prevent infection. Foreign particles close to the skin's surface may be carefully removed with tweezers that have been sterilized over an open flame or boiled in water.

(4) *Do not* attempt to remove any foreign material that is deeply imbedded in a muscle or other tissue as serious bleeding may result. This must be done by a doctor.

(5) Rinse the wound thoroughly under running water.

(6) Pat the wound dry with a sterile or clean cloth.

(7) *Do not* apply ointments, medication, antiseptic spray or home remedies unless told to do so by a doctor.

(8) Cover the wound with a sterile dressing and bandage in place. If the cut is slightly gaping, apply a butterfly bandage (see page 35) or

tape the wound to get the edges as close together as possible.

(9) Always seek medical attention if:
   (a) The wound is severe.
   (b) The bleeding does not stop.
   (c) The injury was caused by an obviously dirty object.
   (d) A foreign material or object is imbedded in the wound.
   (e) Signs of infection such as fever, redness, swelling, increased tenderness at the site of the wound, pus or red streaks leading from the wound toward the body appear.
   (f) There is any doubt about tetanus immunization.

(10) If medical assistance is not readily available and the wound shows signs of infection, keep the victim lying down with the injured area immobilized and elevated. Apply warm wet cloths over the wound until medical assistance can be obtained.

Puncture Wounds

A puncture wound results from a sharp object such as a nail, large splinter, knife, needle, bullet, firecracker, ice pick, etc., piercing the skin and the underlying tissue. The wound is usually deep and narrow with little bleeding. This increases the chance for infection because the germs are not washed out by the flow of blood.

Tetanus is a danger with any wound, but is greater with puncture wounds since the tetanus bacteria grow well in a deep wound where there is little oxygen. *All* puncture injuries should be seen by a doctor.

WHAT TO DO   (1) Wash your hands with soap and water before examining the wound.

(2) Look to see if any part of the offending ob-

ject has broken off and become lodged in the wound.

(3) *Do not* attempt to remove any foreign object that is deeply imbedded in the wound as the foreign object may break off in the wound and/or serious bleeding may result. This must be done by a doctor.

(4) *Do not* poke or put medication into the wound.

(5) In obviously minor puncture wounds, objects sticking in no deeper than the skin's surface may be carefully removed with tweezers that have been sterilized over an open flame or boiled in water.

(6) Encourage bleeding to wash out germs from inside the wound by gently pressing on the edge of the wound.

Do not press so hard as to cause additional injury to the wound.

(7) If the puncture wound is obviously minor, wash the wound with soap and water and rinse under running water.

(8) *Do not* wash large, deep puncture wounds.

(9) Cover the wound with a sterile or clean dressing and bandage in place.

(10) Treat for shock if necessary.

(11) Seek medical attention promptly.

(12) If medical attention is not readily available and the wound shows signs of infection such as fever, redness, swelling, increased tenderness at the site of the wound, pus or red streaks leading from the wound towards the body, see Open Wounds, What To Do, number 10, on page 229.

Scrapes and Scratches

Scrapes can become easily infected since the outer protective skin layer is destroyed in the area.

WHAT TO DO

(1) Wash your hands with soap and water before treating the wound.

(2) Wash the injured area well with soap and water to remove any dirt. Gentle scrubbing may be necessary. It is important to remove all dirt to prevent infection. Bits of dirt left in the wound may also cause permanent discoloration of the skin. Rinse the wound under running water.

(3) *Do not* put medication on the wound unless so directed by a doctor.

(4) Minor scrapes and scratches can be left exposed to the air. Cover larger wounds or those likely to be reinjured with a sterile pad or clean cloth and bandage in place.

(5) Watch for signs of infection. (See Open Wounds, What To Do, number 10, on page 229).

(6) Seek medical attention if the wound is large or deep or there is a question of tetanus immunization.

Special Wounds

Chest Wound

In a deep open chest wound, damage to the lungs may occur, resulting in air flowing in and out of the wound with breathing and not in and out of the lungs where it is needed. This is a serious emergency.

IMMEDIATE TREATMENT

(1) *Do not* remove any object remaining in the wound as *very* serious bleeding or other internal life-threatening problems may result.

(2) Immediately cover the *entire* wound with a pad such as dry sterile gauze (preferably), a clean cloth, clothing, plastic wrap, aluminum foil or other suitable material. The pad *must* be large enough to cover the entire wound and must be airtight so that air will not escape.

(3) If no pad is available, place a hand on each side of the wound and firmly push the skin together to close the wound.

(4) Apply an airtight bandage with tape or other suitable material if available.

(5) Maintain an open airway and restore breathing if necessary.

(6) Treat the victim for shock. It may be necessary to slightly raise the victim's shoulders to aid breathing.

(7) *Do not* give the victim anything to eat or drink as this may cause choking. Also, the stomach should be empty in case surgery is necessary.

(8) Reassure the victim. Gentleness, kindness and understanding play an important role in treating a victim in shock.

(9) Seek medical attention immediately at the nearest hospital emergency room.

Abdominal Wound

Deep abdominal wounds are an emergency. Surgery will probably be necessary to repair the wound.

IMMEDIATE TREATMENT

(1) Maintain an open airway and restore breathing if necessary.

(2) Keep the victim lying down on his back.

(3) Bend the victim's legs at his knees and place a pillow, rolled towel, blanket, clothing, etc., under his knees to relax the abdominal muscles.

(4) Apply direct pressure if necessary to control bleeding. (See Bleeding, Immediate Treatment, pages 73–77.) The abdomen is soft and pressure decreases or stops internal bleeding.

(5) *Do not* try to push intestines back in place if they are sticking out of the wound.

(6) If medical assistance is not readily available and the intestine is sticking out of the

wound, dampen a pad with sterile or boiled and *then cooled* water, if available. Drinking water or clean seawater may be used in an emergency. Place this damp pad over the intestine.

(7) Cover the *entire* wound with a sterile pad such as gauze (preferably), or a clean cloth, clothing, towel, plastic wrap, aluminum foil or other suitable material.

(8) Apply a firm bandage to hold the pad in place. Do not bandage too tightly.

(9) Keep the victim comfortably warm.

(10) *Do not* give the victim anything to eat or drink, including water, as surgery will proba bly be necessary and the stomach should be empty.

(11) Seek medical attention immediately at the nearest hospital emergency room.

CLOSED WOUND

Closed wounds are not always obvious as there is no break in the skin. Suspect internal wounds if the victim has been in an accident, fallen or received a severe body blow to chest, abdomen, head, spine, etc. Internal injuries may be very serious.

SYMPTOMS

(1) Pain and tenderness at the site of the injury. Redness of the skin where blow occurred.

(2) Vomit that resembles coffee grounds.

(3) Coughed up blood that is bright red.

(4) Stools containing dark, tarry material or bright red blood.

(5) Urine containing blood.

(6) Pale skin.

(7) Cold clammy skin.

(8) Rapid but weak pulse.

(9) Rapid breathing.

(10) Dizziness.

(11) Swelling.
(12) Restlessness.
(13) Thirst.

IMMEDIATE TREATMENT

(1) Maintain an open airway and restore breathing if necessary.
(2) Seek medical attention promptly.

CONTINUED CARE

(1) Keep the victim lying down and quiet.
(2) If the victim is vomiting, turn his head to the side to prevent choking.
(3) If the victim has difficulty with breathing, raise his shoulders with a pillow.
(4) Check for other injuries, such as broken bones, and administer treatment.
(5) Keep the victim comfortably warm.
(6) *Do not* give the victim anything to eat or drink, including water.
(7) Reassure the victim. Gentleness, kindness and understanding play an important role in treating a victim of any injury or illness.
(8) If the victim must be moved by someone other than trained medical personnel, keep the victim lying down and be very careful.
See Also: Bleeding; Broken Bones and Spinal Injuries; Head Injuries; Shock

● **Wrist injury:** see Broken Bones and Spinal Injuries; Sprains

Family Members (Names)	Allergies	DPT	Tetanus Booster	Measles	Mumps	
Father						
Mother						
Children/Other						

BOOSTER—DATES

Rubella	Polio	Major Medical Problems	Medication Taken Regularly	Other Medical Information

ABOUT THE AUTHORS

MARTHA ROSS FRANKS is a medical writer who lives in suburban Chicago. She has written extensively for AMA publications and was formerly North Central States editor of a national medical newsletter. Marti was born in 1943 in Charlotte, North Carolina, and received her B.A. degree in economics in 1965 from Salem College (Winston-Salem, North Carolina). She is married and the mother of two children.

RICHARD LOWE, the illustrator of this book, is a freelance illustrator who lives in Chicago with his two children. A native of Pea Ridge, Mississippi, he attended the University of Mississippi and Harris School of Advertising Art in Nashville, where he was also an instructor. His illustrations have previously appeared in national magazines.

NOTES

NOTES

NOTES

Personal property of George Wyman